# The Job Search Guide for Recession-Proof Careers

## Strategies to Find Work and Secure Your Career When the Economy Slows

### Jordan Blake

No part of this book may be reproduced or utilized in any form or by any means, electronic or mechanical, including photocopying, recording, or by any information storage and retrieval system, without permission in writing from the publisher.

Copyright © 2025 BY Synast Publishing

Published by Synast Publishing

All rights reserved.

ISBN: 979-8-9929503-9-7

# INTRODUCTION

In an era where economic downturns have become almost cyclical, securing a career that withstands the ebb and flow of financial turbulence is more crucial than ever. The complexities of a shifting job market demand not only resilience but also a strategic approach to career management. This book serves as a comprehensive guide for navigating these challenges, equipping readers with the necessary tools to secure a stable employment path even in the face of economic adversity.

Understanding the dynamics of recession-proof industries is the first step toward career stability. By analyzing historical data and identifying the characteristics of resilient sectors, such as healthcare, technology, and essential services, readers can strategically target job opportunities that offer long-term security. The book delves into emerging fields like renewable energy and cybersecurity, highlighting the potential these areas hold for future growth.

Moreover, the guide emphasizes the importance of adaptability and lifelong learning as cornerstones of a robust career strategy. By cultivating a growth mindset and continuously upgrading skills, professionals can enhance their employability and remain competitive. The book provides actionable insights into skill mapping, cross-industry transitions, and the development of a personal brand that stands out in the crowded job market.

Networking and personal branding are also critical components of this guide. Readers will learn how to leverage platforms like LinkedIn to build professional connections and how to tap into the hidden job market effectively. The book offers practical advice on crafting standout resumes and cover letters, preparing for virtual interviews, and utilizing job search platforms to their fullest potential.

Ultimately, this guide is designed to empower individuals to take control of their career trajectories, providing them with the resilience and foresight needed to thrive in unpredictable economic climates. Through a blend of strategic planning, skill enhancement, and proactive networking, readers are encouraged to build a career foundation that not only survives but flourishes during recessions.

# Table of Contents

Chapter 1: Understanding the Recession-Proof Job Market 1

    Analyzing Industry Resilience ................................. 1

    Identifying High-Demand Sectors ........................... 3

    Exploring Emerging Opportunities .......................... 6

    Evaluating Economic Indicators ............................... 8

    Research Tools for Industry Analysis ..................... 10

Chapter 2: Building a Resilient Career Foundation .......... 13

    Developing Flexibility and Adaptability ................ 13

    Upskilling for Market Demands ............................. 15

    Leveraging Online Learning ..................................... 17

    Creating a Personal Skill Development Plan ........... 19

    Harnessing Technology for Growth ........................ 21

Chapter 3: Mastering Networking Strategies ..................... 24

    Digital Networking Tools ......................................... 24

    Creating Meaningful Virtual Connections ............. 26

    Navigating Industry Events ..................................... 28

    Building Professional Networks ............................. 30

    Leveraging Informational Interviews ..................... 32

Chapter 4: Crafting a Standout Personal Brand ................ 35

    Defining Your Career Narrative .............................. 35

Building an Online Presence ..................................... 37
Utilizing Social Media................................................ 39
Optimizing LinkedIn Profiles................................... 41
Showcasing Expertise Through Content................. 43

Chapter 5: Navigating the Job Search Process ....................46

Tailoring Resumes for Industries............................. 46
Developing Compelling Cover Letters .................... 48
Preparing for Virtual Interviews .............................. 50
Utilizing Job Search Platforms ................................ 51
Exploring the Hidden Job Market............................ 53

Chapter 6: Avoiding Common Job Search Pitfalls..............56

Identifying Common Mistakes................................. 56
Developing a Strategic Plan ..................................... 58
Maintaining Persistence and Resilience.................. 60
Overcoming Job Search Challenges......................... 62
Building Emotional Resilience................................. 64

Chapter 7: Transitioning Between Industries .....................67

Assessing Transferable Skills ................................... 67
Exploring Cross-Industry Opportunities................ 69
Developing a Transition Action Plan ...................... 71
Navigating Salary Adjustments ............................... 73
Building Confidence for Career Pivots.................... 75

Chapter 8: Leveraging Mentorship and Support................80

Finding and Building Mentor Relationships..........80
Engaging in Professional Communities .................82
Utilizing Mentorship in Transitions .......................84
Developing Support Systems....................................86
Real-World Mentorship Success Stories.................88

Chapter 9: Preparing for the Future of Work .....................91
Embracing Remote Work..........................................91
Focusing on Emerging Technologies.....................93
Anticipating Industry Trends ..................................95
Building Long-term Career Resilience...................97
Creating a Vision for Your Career ........................100

Chapter 10: Cultivating Lifelong Learning Habits .......... 102
Importance of Continuous Learning ....................102
Developing Learning Routines ..............................104
Role of Curiosity in Learning.................................106
Lifelong Learning Success Stories.........................108
Incorporating Learning into Daily Life................110

Chapter 11: Balancing Career and Personal Well-being 113
Importance of Work-Life Balance.........................113
Prioritizing Health and Well-being.......................115
Aligning Career with Personal Values .................117
Examples of Balanced Success ..............................119
Strategies for Maintaining Balance.......................121

Chapter 12: Staying Motivated Through Setbacks .......... 124

Psychological Impact of Rejection ......................... 124
Building Resilience Against Rejections ................. 126
Rebounding from Setbacks ..................................... 128
Stories of Resilience and Perseverance .................. 130
Maintaining Motivation .......................................... 132

## Chapter 13: Aligning Career Goals with Market Demands 135

Goal Setting Based on Market Needs ..................... 135
Importance of Lifelong Learning ............................ 137
Tools for Career Alignment ..................................... 139
Personal Development Strategies ........................... 141
Examples of Effective Goal Setting ........................ 144

## Chapter 14: Navigating Industry Disruptions and Opportunities
................................................................................ 146

Key Industry Disruptions ........................................ 146
Opportunities from Disruptions .............................. 148
Responding to Industry Changes ............................ 150
Adaptive Career Examples ..................................... 152
Aligning Goals with Market Demands ................... 154

## Chapter 15: Harnessing Technology for Career Success 157

Exploring Technological Tools ............................... 157
Using Technology for Networking ......................... 159
Technology for Skill Enhancement ........................ 161
Staying Updated with Tech Trends ........................ 163
Examples of Tech-Driven Career Growth ............. 165

# Chapter 1: Understanding the Recession-Proof Job Market

## Analyzing Industry Resilience

It is essential in times of economic uncertainty to know which industries can survive downturns to maintain career stability. Industry resilience is about some sectors keeping steady and even improving when an economic recession occurs. The firms in these industries sustain their operations mainly because of their key functions, permanent demand, and policies that allow them to keep running in any situation.

Examining how industries coped during earlier recessions provides insights that help people decide what to do now. Healthcare and pharmaceuticals have often remained strong since medical services and products are always needed. Likewise, water, electricity, and gas services in the utilities sector are always required to help keep the industry stable in bad economic times. It shows great strength in difficult times, mainly due to constant innovation and the fact businesses are turning more to digital solutions.

Industry resilience also depends on having goods purchased by consumers all year. No matter what the economy looks like, these items are products that are regularly purchased, such as essentials such as food and household items. In difficult economic times, the employment offered by industries that make these goods is usually less likely to fluctuate.

Furthermore, many emerging sectors demonstrate remarkable resilience, especially as they are closely related to worldwide trends and what the future needs. Because sustainable actions are gaining importance, there is now increased interest in renewable energy and its growth and stability. Rapid digital changes have made cybersecurity a rapidly developing area focused on keeping data safe. These areas ensure stability and, at the same time, supply options for progress and new ideas.

Individuals need to rely on various helpful tools and resources in order to choose recession-proof industries. Values from government labor statistics help us understand how multiple industries are doing and what new jobs are available, while market forecasts indicate sectors that seem the most steady. Examining information such as GDP growth, unemployment, and how confident consumers are can help you realize the effect of the broader economy on people's jobs.

We should not miss how forces like globalization and technology influence this industry. Both international trade agreements and technological progress tend to change different industries and offer new opportunities and issues. Knowledge of these dynamics allows us to find sectors that are both tough and positioned for future growth.

Overall, an industry's resilience is studied by using a mix of its past achievements, inherited traits, and recent noteworthy developments. People who work in essential services, continuing products, and areas that will matter moving forward are more likely to succeed and stay employed during economic slowdowns. Acting on this strategy allows job seekers to make decisions that improve their ability to succeed in different financial circumstances.

## Identifying High-Demand Sectors

Since the job market can change rapidly, people need to look for areas that will give them stability during tough economic times. Such working fields are well-positioned to survive recessions and provide job security for people wanting strong careers.

To spot high-demand areas, we must first identify what helps them resist changes and challenges. For example, unlike many goods, non-cyclical consumer goods experience regular demand no matter how the economy changes. Among these are the basics you need every day, such as food, drinks, and products used around the house. Because these goods are always needed, industries relying on them don't face significant challenges during economic declines.

Recession-proof businesses often depend on key services. Emergency healthcare, utilities, and public safety services are needed, rain or shine. According to Market Research Watch, the healthcare field is growing thanks to an aging population and new scientific discoveries in medicine. Water, electricity, and waste management are also essential, as people and companies need them daily.

The influence of strict rules is another essential part of understanding prospering industrial sectors. Specific industries operate more smoothly thanks to regulations and laws that support their demands. Thanks to environmental laws, businesses in renewable energy have expanded as nations globally aim for greener solutions and lower emissions. Because of such regulations, not only is growth more stable in these areas, but it also speeds up, leading to many new jobs in solar and wind energy.

As technology and globalization have appeared, they have also brought about demand for new types of work. Because digital infrastructures need more protection from cyber threats, cybersecurity has experienced swift growth. Relying more on technology, many large organizations now require cybersecurity experts.

Also, the world's move towards digital transformation has made newer paths in technology-focused sectors. Demand for data analytics, artificial intelligence, and software developers has grown as businesses try to use data to make crucial decisions and streamline work.

Job seekers must make sure they have the right resources and tools to find out which areas are in great demand. As a result, government labor statistics can supply important information about industry growth and future job prospects. Reviewing industry and market outlooks allows you to spot which parts of the economy will grow. They give people the information they need to choose a career that matches their skills and the requirements of the labor market.

Noticing economic trends matters a lot when planning your career. To predict what will happen in the job market, we must look at indicators such as GDP, unemployment rates, and what people think about their finances. Acknowledging the factors in these indicators helps guide a person's career successfully when the economy is slowing down.

You should use your market knowledge, rely on facts and statistics, and match your talents with the needs of growing sectors. Finding areas that are strong and have room for growth gives job seekers chances to create a career that can handle tough economic times.

## Exploring Emerging Opportunities

The kinds of careers available today are affected by new technologies, shifts in society, and alterations in the economy. Because of issues in traditional industries, new careers are becoming available in new sectors. Because things change fast in the workforce, spotting these emerging opportunities is vital to your job stability.

The renewable energy sector is exhibiting some of the most significant GDP increases. As more people worry about the environment, sustainable energy solutions are gaining more substantial support. Because of these changes, there is now a need for experts who are knowledgeable about solar, wind, and similar technologies. Experts in this field benefit from stability and are dedicated to progress in sustainable development around the world. The move from using fossil fuels to renewable energy is not simply fashionable but essential and opens doors to jobs in engineering, project management, and environmental consultancy.

A fast-growing area of importance is cybersecurity. As so many things are done online these days, having strict cybersecurity protections is more necessary than ever. Companies are putting plenty of resources into cybersecurity to maintain customer trust and secure their data. With this, many businesses and industries have hired more cybersecurity specialists; tasks include both security analysis and ethical hacking. Because they're so necessary, these jobs are safe from downturns and also provide room to learn and grow as technology advances.

Healthcare technology is expanding at a breakneck pace. When technology is combined with healthcare, both patient treatment and business operations change. Resources and procedures are influencing medical practices. Experts who work at the junction of healthcare and technology are valued, as they help make healthcare systems more productive and effective.

The explosion of Uber, Airbnb, and online freelance sites has led to gig work that is flexible and allows you to do different kinds of jobs. Since freelance work isn't as stable as a regular job, it helps people to have more than one income and enhance their skills. The gig workforce is more attractive when the economy is weak because it gives people more stable work. People who select gigs that support their career ambitions can use this pattern to grow a flexible and strong career.

Taking action today is essential for becoming aware of new job opportunities. You need to understand the latest industry happenings, keep educating yourself, and be willing to move into different fields. Networking helps greatly by showing you what's trending in the industry and what options you have for your career. Joining industry gatherings, attending online webinars, and networking allows people to gain practical knowledge that can help them plan their careers.

To do well in a constantly evolving job market, you have to be able to spot new chances and respond to them. If individuals choose growth areas and use their abilities and interests to meet what the market requires, they can succeed in their jobs and help shape the industries ahead.

## Evaluating Economic Indicators

Being aware of economic indicators is necessary for anyone trying to find work when the economy is acting unpredictably. It is easy to see the condition and course of the economy by examining economic factors like GDP, unemployment rates, and how people feel confident about their spending. They show how various areas might do and, as a result, where people might find or lose job opportunities.

Experts often agree that GDP is the best indicator of how well an economy is doing. It's the sum of all goods and services produced in a specific period in a country. The expansion of the GDP often means there are more jobs and the economy is strong, whereas a reduction could mean people may lose work and the economy is weak. Watching trends in GDP can help people considering a career choose where there is more activity and less.

Another vital index, the unemployment rate, shows how the labor market was doing at the time. Many unemployed people may be because job availability is rare and competition is severe.

On the contrary, whenever unemployment is low, there are plenty of chances for those seeking work. Information from the report can show people looking for employment, the industries with the most available work, and the areas that require the most workers.

The consumer confidence index evaluates the level of positive feelings consumers have about both the economy and their finances. Higher consumer confidence usually means people spend and invest more, which boosts the economy and encourages job creation. Consequently, low confidence among buyers may lessen their spending, limit the power of the economy, and make it harder to keep jobs safe. If job seekers closely track how consumers feel these days, they will be able to expect economic changes and change their approach to work.

In addition to the standard indicators, globalization, and technological progress play a big part in defining current economic issues and labor markets. Trade and economic deals at the global level can truly alter local areas, changing work in industry and service sectors alike. Just as technology can start new industries, it often leads to the transformation of older ones, bringing about new kinds of work and demanding workers to gain different skills.

Navigating a career often means you need to pay close attention to economic indicators and the broader economy. It helps individuals see shifts in the job market and guides them to develop skills matching the latest opportunities. Being proactive in your career can help keep your job and make you more satisfied at work during challenging economic times.

Adding trend analysis to how you plan your career is a wise choice. Using market trends can help individuals guess the direction of job availability and learn what skills are most needed. Thanks to this predictive ability, job seekers strive to match their skills with what employers will need ahead, giving them an edge when things get tough economically.

Interpreting what the numbers tell us is essential for our job prospects. Those who remain current and flexible can deal more effectively with the problems in the job market, no matter what happens in the economy. Because of this knowledge, individuals can choose their careers skillfully, adapt to changes, and do well at work.

## Research Tools for Industry Analysis

In order to discover recession-proof job prospects, you need to learn the proper tools and techniques for industry analysis. A person needs to make use of both old and new research tools to gain a good understanding of industry patterns and economic signals in this environment.

To begin, it is helpful to use government labor statistics. These statistics, usually made public by national labor departments, supply a lot of information about employment, expanding industries, and shifts among populations. Studying these statistics allows people looking for work to pick industries that are growing and provide job security.

Besides, industry reports and forecasts are highly beneficial. These reports from market research companies analyze certain industries, point to important actors, and foresee upcoming developments and disruptive changes. Individuals planning for a strong career in tech should make sure they are aware of these reports. They give an idea of what's to come, guiding people to adjust and add new abilities.

In addition, industry analysis depends greatly on statistics like GDP, the rate of unemployment, and consumer loyalty to brands. They represent the state of the economy and can greatly change job opportunities. A high GDP is typically followed by economic progress, often bringing about more employment opportunities in several areas. In such situations, when unemployment is higher, there are usually fewer job openings, so you should be more careful when making decisions about your career.

Industry dynamics are strongly affected by new technological developments. The shift to digital technologies has greatly transformed how industry analysis is performed. You can find a lot of industry information and analysis from online sources like Statista and IBISWorld. Because of these websites, users can study and compare many sectors, making it simpler to make the best decisions.

To analyze industries, businesses are increasingly depending on social media and LinkedIn. People who follow what industry groups do and listen to thought leaders can learn about the newest trends and developments. Through these platforms, people can take part in immediate discussions and webinars, which give them a clearer view of industry changes.

People interested in studying a particular field can discover firsthand knowledge by joining industry-related conferences or seminars. These occasions connect industry leaders and help attendees exchange ideas and build relationships. Participants may obtain useful information about challenges and innovations in the industry to help them choose their future careers.

Seeing real cases and situation-based examples of industries shows the answers to this question in real life. An individual can learn how to cope with hard times and grow by examining the methods companies use during tough economic or technological phases.

Successfully working with such tools to carry out industry analysis is crucial for anyone seeking a career protected from recession. By looking at statistics, future market trends, economic signals, and technology, job applicants can develop a clear strategy for the job market. Using this method, someone can learn about what is happening in the industry now and get ready for what lies ahead.

# Chapter 2: Building a Resilient Career Foundation

## Developing Flexibility and Adaptability

Today, being flexible and adaptable is very important for a successful business career when industries and tech progress, people in these industries should be ready to change their jobs and handle these changes positively.

A flexible person is capable of moving from one area of an organization to another according to their needs. Part of this may be learning new tasks that are not usual for your role or working under a new company structure. Instead of seeing shifts as dangers, employees should regard them as opportunities to increase their skills. Taking on new responsibilities helps individuals continue to benefit their bosses, even during times when the economy is not certain.

The key part of adaptability is the willingness to rethink your strategies and way of thinking to respond to what is happening around you. For example, it could require you to be flexible about advice, willing to learn from others, and open to learning skills not linked to your usual job area. Openness to learning new things encourages you to attend courses, earn certificates, and value experiences like being mentored and working with others.

Opening your mind to continuous improvement is one way to be flexible and adapt. Managers must follow industry trends as well as drop outdated methods when they learn about better ones. If we can look at problems as chances to solve them creatively rather than as something to fear, we are more adaptable.

Flexible people often show these skills by taking part in projects that include workers from several departments and involve using their skills in ways they haven't before. As well as learning new abilities, these situations help earn a reputation as someone who brings value to any team.

The importance of soft skills in helping people adapt is very high. Abilities such as good communication, active listening, and creative problem-solving are important for dealing with today's often changing and challenging work situations. Thanks to these skills, people can cooperate, accept feedback positively, and find fresh ways to solve problems.

Being flexible and adaptable means you are better ready for what comes your way and can make the most of any new chance when given. Because of this, professionals have careers that are strong and able to bear whatever changes occur. Learning new things and remaining open to change allow people to work well in the fast-changing job market and feel safe about their careers.

## Upskilling for Market Demands

As careers continue to adapt, being able to update and improve your abilities is very important. As businesses keep advancing and new technology gets introduced, what people should learn may also change fast, so professionals must be ready for these changes. The beginning of this journey is to see which skills are most valuable in different sectors. With so much happening online, companies now require data analysis, digital marketing, and social media management skills.

The key to this process is analyzing the skill gap. Anyone should take time to examine their skills and find where there are gaps. Here, sharing your work with peers and mentors allows them to give useful suggestions for your progress. As soon as these gaps are recognized, professionals can plan learning goals that follow what the market is looking for.

There are now more ways to learn new skills than ever before because of online learning sites. A good approach is to participate in certified online programs and go to workshops and seminars for your career. These sites feature many different courses, which helps learners choose what suits their career interests.

Yet, understanding concepts alone isn't enough. To make learning last and prove your skills, you must practice using them in hands-on ways. Participating in paid projects or giving your time to volunteer work helps develop your skills and allows you to present your abilities to employers.

To use online learning platforms in the best way, you must plan your actions. Choosing the right classes from many choices is very important. Part of the process is matching the course material to current market trends and assessing both the instructors and the feedback given by previous students. Effective use of online education requires you to have a scheduled study routine and actively participate in conversations within the course community.

Many people have managed to change their careers by studying online. Marketing professionals who shift to data analytics and teachers learning about educational technology are good examples of how upskilling can result in new careers. They give us reasons to commit to discovering new skills and adapting to changes in the workplace.

Creating a plan for your personal skill development is an organized way to help you learn new things. This process starts with setting achievable objectives and then tracking student advancements all the way through. A clearly outlined plan lists both short-term and long-term goals, helping you learn what you need to know. Blending taking online courses with going to in-person workshops or following the work of real professionals ensures the learning process is always engaging and broad.

In addition, having digital planners and skills journals to watch progress encourages people to stay motivated. People who manage their achievements and areas for progress maintain their career growth and adjust well to market changes. This initiative to improve skills helps people get hired and prepares them well to deal with unpredictable job openings.

## Leveraging Online Learning

Today, using online learning platforms has become essential for people trying to be more resilient and better prepared for job changes. Because of so many online educational resources, you can find and take a wide variety of courses and receive certificates that fit many different interests and skill levels. Because information is accessible to all, individuals can regularly update what they know and do to stay in line with the changing needs of their workplace.

Because of online learning platforms, Coursera and LinkedIn Learning, individuals have new opportunities to learn skills. With these sites, you can find a variety of courses, mainly made by universities and professionals in their fields, which provide superior learning experiences. Being able to learn online at your own pace means people can match their studies to the demands of their jobs and other responsibilities. Those currently employed or with family duties can benefit most from this adaptability since they don't have to make substantial changes to attend classes.

Picking the right courses plays a key role in making sure you take full advantage of online learning. Learners must match their course choices to where they want their careers to head and what is happening in the industry presently. You should judge the credibility of those teaching and the importance of the course content to make better choices. Being involved in forums and chat groups in your course can help you meet different ideas and expand your learning.

The good results seen from using online learning can be seen in how individuals adjust their careers or improve in their areas of expertise. People in marketing who decide to enter data analytics have turned to online courses to get the necessary technical education required to feel confident in their new jobs. Meanwhile, teachers who build their expertise in educational technology find that online programs focused on certain skills help them add digital tools to their educational methods.

A planned strategy for improving skills is necessary for everyone to take advantage of online learning. A personal development plan helps you determine what you want to learn, plan daily activities, and follow your improvement. By following this method, learners are able to stay determined and gather the skills they need in their jobs. Mixing different learning methods, online courses combined with in-person seminars brings the best of both worlds, as well as new skills practice.

Overall, making the most of online tools can strongly improve your ability to deal with changes in the workplace. Regular learning and tying study efforts to career plans give people a strong edge in today's tough job market. By learning new skills and information online, individuals help their careers and also develop a lifelong need to acquire new knowledge needed for today's job market.

## Creating a Personal Skill Development Plan

Designing your skill development plan is critical for growing your career and guaranteeing you are up-to-date in your field as it develops. You should first realize that using a systematic method for gaining skills leads to effective learning and a path that matches what you hope to achieve in your career.

A good skill development plan is built on setting easy-to-reach and well-defined learning goals. You should look at what your future employment prospects may be and what your next five years might look like. You may focus on studying for short-term certificates that can be applied in your workplace right away. Long-term goals could be about nurturing abilities that fit future opportunities in the worker's career.

As soon as goals are decided, making a schedule for gaining those needed skills matters greatly. With the help of the timeline, learners can follow the appropriate learning process and verify that their achievements are supported by continuous progress. It helps students divide their learning aims into smaller chunks, which leads to smaller steps forward.

Using a range of learning techniques is also very important in a skill development plan. Taking a multi-part approach makes learning fun and complete for students. You can mix online lessons, in-person workshops, and chances to observe professionals at work or join related projects. Variety among students provides a richer learning process and is also helpful for anyone with different learning preferences.

Keeping an eye on how you are getting along is essential to keep yourself motivated. There are many tools and resources available to help you follow your skill progress. Depending on digital planners or applications help students organize and schedule their assignments properly. Creating a skills journal or portfolio gives individuals a way to notice their development and remember their experiences.

Technology is now an essential part of today's plans for skill development. Online learning platforms such as Coursera or LinkedIn Learning give access to countless courses meant for people chasing their career ambitions. Most online courses are developed along with industry professionals and educational institutions for their reality and usefulness.

Furthermore, technology makes it easier for students to apply new learning. Using training modules or simulations over the internet can allow you to be involved in practical exercises, filling the space between book learning and real situations.

To maintain the importance of a skill development plan, professionals should pay attention to new industry developments and technological advancements. Updating the learning plan from time to time makes sure its objectives are closely related to what the market requires. By taking this initiative, people increase their ability to adapt to their jobs and are ready to catch new opportunities in their industry.

All in all, building a personal skill development plan includes planning, using many different methods to learn, and adapting continuously to new rules in your field. If people set specific targets, use a range of learning tools, and use technology well, they are more likely to achieve success in their careers.

## Harnessing Technology for Growth

Technology is now one of the leading forces that is helping to create growth and new ideas in every field. By using technology well, individuals can simplify their workflows, talk with others more easily, and create new ways to move up in their jobs. A major way technology helps with a career is by providing tools that make workers more efficient. Using Trello or Asana allows teams to manage their work more efficiently and helps keep projects on schedule. Since Slack and Microsoft Teams are online communication platforms, they make it much easier for workers from various places to join in daily team tasks. Using these tools makes staff more productive and inspires them to work together, which can bring about brilliant ideas.

Career growth today is largely impacted by improved networking, which has resulted from new technologies. Social networks like LinkedIn have changed the way people get in touch with peers in the field, potential hirers, and mentors. Updating a LinkedIn profile allows people to prove their qualifications, give advice, network worldwide, and open up new career ventures. Interacting at virtual events and attending webinars gives professionals extra opportunities to learn from experts in their sector.

Technology also helps create good opportunities for continuous learning. Now that Coursera and LinkedIn Learning exist, individuals are able to enroll in many courses that help them with their career plans. Using these platforms, professionals can obtain new skills when they fit their schedule, which helps them balance work and study. Attending webinars and podcasts on relevant topics helps professionals know about fresh trends and changes within the industry.

Because technology is now present in many industries, new work opportunities have appeared. Healthcare is changing thanks to telemedicine and digital records, which has led to a rise in demand for people who know about health informatics and digital health technology. Just like the financial services sector, those who understand digital financial services can take advantage of the new opportunities that arise from the adoption of fintech solutions. If individuals in the industry keep up with technology, they are more likely to get roles that are satisfying and not at risk when there is a recession.

It is necessary to keep track of technological progress to help your career. Professionals should frequently check tech news, subscribe to appropriate publications, and join technology conferences and expos. Doing this helps them stay ahead and be ready for changes within their profession.

Essentially, technology helps drive our careers forward. If they use social media effectively, individuals can get more done, connect with others, and keep improving their skills for jobs in a fast-changing world. Actively using technology in their careers will allow professionals to manage future problems and take advantage of new work opportunities.

# Chapter 3: Mastering Networking Strategies

## Digital Networking Tools

Today, with digital advancements, making and maintaining professional relationships has broken through past barriers. Because of technology in networking, professionals now interact, exchange information, and take advantage of opportunities in new ways. Networking in the digital era is made easy and flexible by various tools that each have special benefits.

A top platform in digital networking is LinkedIn. This website makes it easy for people to form professional connections by showcasing their experience, skills, and accomplishments in their careers. On LinkedIn, it is possible for people to meet colleagues and leaders in their industry and also take part in groups that fit their career interests. In these groups, people have opportunities to discuss, share knowledge, and form partnerships that may improve their careers.

Most people think of Twitter as a place for friendly chat, but it's also an important tool for professional connections.

Through LinkedIn, users can watch live updates and valuable thoughts shared by leaders from the field. Using hashtags and Twitter chats, professionals can reach more people and be seen by a broader audience in their sector. If you are interested in becoming influential in your field, LinkedIn is very useful for posting and chatting about industry matters.

For anyone interested in making local connections, Meetup provides a special way to do so. It allows users to be involved with current events and programs that support their careers. Whether you go to a meetup, a workshop, or a seminar, you can network in person and build important work relationships or find new job openings.

Networking successfully now depends on how well you maintain your online presence. A properly set up LinkedIn profile is a big help for career development. It should consist of a headshot, a short overview listing key abilities and successes, and statements of approval from both clients and colleagues. Using the correct keywords on your profile can help you appear in more searches, so employers and fellow researchers are more likely to find you.

Having an online account is not enough; you also need to join in on activities on digital platforms. You can make your presence known in the professional community by sharing articles connected to your industry, leaving comments, and starting engagements on posts. By engaging actively, content creators can grow their brand that is authentic and shows their skills.

Connecting with professionals can be managed more easily with specialized tools meant to keep your professional network organized. Apps such as Nimble are designed to make sure you never overlook people you have connected with. By using scheduling software, it's easier to stay in regular touch with contacts and develop lasting relationships.

Digital networks are always changing and develop over time. Using the newest equipment and practices is important to make the most out of your digital network. If you utilize these tools efficiently, you will build a reliable network to help your career thrive in a tough job environment.

## Creating Meaningful Virtual Connections

These days, building effective relationships with others online is key to your professional success. The main point in online communication is to build meaningful connections, surpassing simple, shallow talks. If you really care about others' accomplishments, you can build meaningful relationships with them. The success of a LinkedIn message or request can be greatly influenced by tailoring each one to what's important to the user, as well as showing you care about their career.

There are many chances to create valuable ties through online platforms. If you use video calls, you can almost have a real discussion, which can boost how well the conversation goes. It is essential to focus during virtual meetings as that shows you respect what others have to say. It allows us to earn trust and build partnerships that will last longer in the industry.

Aside from conversations with individuals, webinars and online groups are reliable places to meet and network. Linking with others on LinkedIn or taking part in webinars is a good way to get involved, discuss ideas, and prove that you are well informed about your industry. Among other things, these sites let you meet colleagues who are passionate about the same things you are.

A marketing specialist discovered this when, by attending many industry webinars, they were able to build productive relationships with industry leaders. As a result of these actions, engineers grew their network and gained opportunities to join important partnerships and climb the career ladder. In addition, entrepreneurs have networked with other entrepreneurs on mastermind groups online, revealing that virtual platforms can be equally effective at supporting career advancement.

There are online tools for maintaining and running these networks efficiently. The use of Nimble allows users to track their business network, follow up regularly, and stay informed about the latest events. They help people follow a routine for talking, which matters a lot for maintaining strong ties.

To make meaningful connections in virtual areas, you must be honest, use smart approaches, and know how to use technology well. Emphasizing genuine conversations and making use of the right digital tools allows people in a job market to build networks that lead to both short- and long-term success.

## Navigating Industry Events

In the world of career growth, industry events play a key part by bringing together people in the same field to discuss, network, and seek new openings. No matter if they are small workshops or large gatherings, these events promote creative thinking and allow guests to learn about the newest advancements in their fields.

If you are prepared, you will get the most out of your industry events. You need to go through careful planning before attending the conference. You need to find out about the agenda, recognize important speakers, and discover what the event focuses on. Deciding which workshops to attend and who to meet can greatly improve your school-related trip experience. If you set goals such as learning about new technologies or boosting your professional network, you'll know what to focus on during the event.

When I got to the event, the whole place was full of activity. People from different parts of the industry come together, sharing what they have learned along the way. By being so diverse, people can learn more together. Being part of debates and meetings helps attendees learn fresh ideas and reconsider their earlier beliefs. They may also bring up the chance to learn about jobs or business options that were unnoticed before.

The most important advantage of events in any industry is networking. Coming into contact with other students, teachers, and possible partners can make it easier to find new job options. It's important to be sincere and really care about the people you network with. If you engage in valuable conversations, provide your contact information, and send after-event messages related to the event, these connections are likely to develop. Taking these efforts can help a quick connection turn into a lasting professional tie, offering ways to support and collaborate for a long time.

This type of event provides a fine opportunity to demonstrate your knowledge and leadership. Many events let attendees join panel talks, lead workshops, or discuss topics during QandA. They help you become better known within the industry and acknowledged as an expert. Even if you don't present, joining in on discussions can help others see your skills and knowledge in the field.

Industry events help with growth, but they are also often inspirational. Learning about news and advances can inspire people to think of original ideas and motivate them to take action in their work or projects. Seeing the accomplishments of those leading their fields tends to inspire People attending to achieve great things in their professions.

In the end, looking back on what happened at the event is very important. Taking time to note the main ideas, recap them, and think about applying them to your job can completely change your experiences from being at the event. Doing this can point out ways to grow and what to learn in the future, so the value of the event lasts for a long time.

## Building Professional Networks

In addition to other skills, career development needs to connect with a broad group of people. Networking helps people access extra opportunities, new ideas, and partnerships that play a big role in steering their careers. Establishing personal relations with the right people can guide you, support you, and introduce you to bigger opportunities in your career.

To start, it is very important to learn how networking works. Building relationships instead of just passing out business cards or joining professional groups is an important part of networking. You should aim to build relationships with those higher than you in your industry, such as mentors and industry veterans, as well as peers and recruiters. Every relationship has the possibility of giving you different views on market trends, job postings, and career development.

A good approach to building your professional connections is by joining in on industry events and forums. They give people a chance to connect with others in their industry. Attending these events gives individuals the chance to learn about the newest happenings in the industry and present what they specialize in. To benefit from such events, you should have a plan, such as ensuring your intro is short and speaking about more than just the weather.

It is also essential to depend on digital networking techniques today. Social networking sites like LinkedIn give professionals a large space to interact and become more visible. Staying active and interested online can help you find candidates for collaboration or employment. Team discussions, sharing valuable information, and meeting those with similar interests can be very useful for your professional goals.

Networking with informational interviews can give you many benefits. Instead of job interviews, they are chances to learn from people who have backgrounds in your fields of interest. The knowledge gained from these interviews can show you different types of jobs, company cultures, and what is expected in your field if you ever want to switch careers.

It is very important to build up a collection of contacts when major changes happen in your professional life. No matter the type of change you face, having a network to recommend, connect you, and advise you can make the transition less stressful. Paying attention to mentors, people already involved in the industry, and specialized recruiters is important for dealing with these changes.

Networking doesn't stop after building it—valuing and upkeeping the relationships you have is just as paramount. Sticking to follow-ups, mercifully saying thanks, and being helpful when you can are key ways to maintain enduring business relationships. You should be sincerely interested in what the other person does and anything they have accomplished when interacting.

Overall, growing your professional network is about forming a network of people who help you in your job. Regular dedication, truthfulness, and well-planned activity are necessary. When a network is well-developed, it introduces many new opportunities and also encourages continual education. When jobs and industries are always changing, people who are good at networking usually adjust best.

## Leveraging Informational Interviews

Talking to someone in an informational interview gives people interested in a different profession or sector key insights. The purpose of these talks is to obtain inside knowledge of the profession or industry and not to find work. They link those thinking about their career with qualified professionals who can give descriptions of their work, difficulties, and rewards.

An informational interview is mostly about learning more about a certain industry or position. With this method, individuals can learn about several careers, get familiar with company expectations and culture, and find out how far their roles can progress. It gives you an opportunity to ask things that job descriptions or interviews might not cover, like how often you would be working, your work-family balance, and which skills matter most in the industry.

You should approach informational interviews in a planned way. First, find the right people to talk to, either experts, former students, or other industry contacts. A polite and simple message at the start helps the conversation go smoothly. You should mention why you are having the meeting, show interest in the work of the professional, and suggest a few different times as possible.

As soon as you have an informational interview, getting prepared helps you make the most out of it. It means finding out more about the person and their company and making sure you have considered questions ahead of time. You should ask questions that can't be answered with yes or no to get thorough answers on different topics. Note-taking in an interview allows you to store valuable ideas and things to follow up on later.

Being thankful is very important in this type of interview. After the meeting, send a thank-you note expressing appreciation for what the person did and for helping to keep you connected in the future. Such a small act might be remembered for years and may help start other helpful conversations or provide opportunities later.

Real cases of people completing successful informational interviews can be found everywhere. A new graduate may hire a mentor who helps them maneuver the beginning of their career. Just like a student, a working professional may learn about a new interest or position through these conversations and improve their work life.

You can participate in professional groups and forums by using informational interviews. People involved in LinkedIn networks can discuss their experiences, seek help, and prove their expertise to others. Connecting this way can help you find unique job postings and the chance to collaborate with others since these may not be detected using standard job search methods.

To sum up, taking part in informational interviews guides you in learning about different careers and developing personally and professionally. It gives you lots of knowledge and helps connect you with others who can support your career, making it important for those wanting to become recession-proof.

# Chapter 4: Crafting a Standout Personal Brand

## Defining Your Career Narrative

Creating a professional story helps someone define and achieve their goals in their career. The narrative ties together important achievements, abilities, and ambitions to show what a person's career path has been like. Not only does this narrative allow you to set your personal and professional goals, but it also lets you explain them effectively to other people.

Introspection and a review of your experiences are the first steps in making your career narrative. It requires noticing times in life that have developed your personal and professional skills. Such moments include making great progress, overcoming difficulties, or experiencing events that direct a person's career. Emphasizing these highlights can allow someone to notice patterns and kinds of experiences they keep having in their work life.

A good career narrative helps you see how your history influences your future ambitions. It helps you move from the past into your future career, linking what you've achieved with your future goals. Making this connection supports the idea that someone's career path follows a clear and connected plan. It clears up doubts and shows people what to do when they encounter future challenges and opportunities.

If you want to craft a satisfying career narrative, make sure your storytelling method engages and resonates with those you are talking to. You should write directly, include engaging details, and put a value on your interests and goals. Listing duties and job experiences alone does not make a story, but it should share your interests and your dreams for the future. It should be faithful to the truth and clear about errors so that no false details tarnish the message.

A strong professional story relies on being genuine. By being honest about themselves and their stories, people gain the trust of their audience. You should accept what you've achieved and what you've faced and explain how these experiences have shaped your development. An honest story fits in with your personal and job goals so potential employees relate to it and find it in line with the company's culture.

Many great career stories highlight hard work and how someone has changed. They narrate ways people have reshaped their career paths, handled change, and improved their focus. They demonstrate creativity, strong leadership, and flexibility, traits that are greatly respected in modern careers. By sharing their stories, individuals help others and show how well they deal with change.

In essence, making a career narrative involves looking back, being artistic, and being real. It offers great advantages for showcasing your brand, planning your career, and reaching out to others professionally. A firm narrative also improves your knowledge of yourself, raises your confidence, and sets you up to prosper in your area of work. A solid career story will still be very valuable as the job market evolves and gets more challenging.

## Building an Online Presence

Because everything is connected today, every person hoping to find a recession-proof career must build a strong web presence. Developing an online presence that matches who you are professionally can lead to opportunities in many different industries. You should begin by selecting and shaping your online identity to fit both your job goals and what is important to you.

Your online presence is built around your professional website. A resume displays your expertise, experience, and achievements to those who may want to work with you or hire you. Be sure to make your website simple in design. Remember to put your contact details on your website and include your best examples in a separate portfolio section. In this way, you both prove your competence and help show off your knowledge.

Besides a website, producing quality content will help you become known as an expert in your field. Sharing your thoughts and findings about industry changes in your blog can make your brand more easily recognizable and respected. Educating others through either articles or whitepapers proves to others that you are knowledgeable and gives you something to show in your professional story. Using digital forums or hosting webinars is a useful way to reach people who aren't present during your training.

Social media helps you promote your professional identity. You can't go wrong with LinkedIn for networking and finding a job. It's important to use your profile to tell your career story and point out the most important things you have achieved and the skills you possess. Share useful articles, join discussions, and network with your industry colleagues. It both helps you establish new connections and makes you aware of what's happening in your field.

In addition, you can connect with others in the industry on Twitter and post your creative samples on Instagram. It gives you the chance to connect and collaborate with other people and influential users instantly. If you are a creative professional, Instagram is the best platform to feature your work and become noticed.

Increasing the number of subscribers to your newsletter is a helpful method to keep your audience involved. By creating newsletters, you can regularly give subscribers updates on what is new and interesting to you. Staying in touch this often with your followers helps you create strong relationships and loyal fans.

Being careful with your online activity helps keep your online presence looking good. Check your online presence and publications now and then to ensure they line up with what matters to you. It means deleting old information you no longer need and updating your privacy permissions to keep your online privacy safe.

If you build your online presence with a plan, you improve your career image and ensure stability during unpredictable economic changes. Your digital footprint will help you keep up and succeed in the job market, which changes all the time.

## Utilizing Social Media

Today, social media is very important, especially for building a career and your professional image. Being on social media can boost your career image and introduce you to more opportunities at work. Effective use of social media can make a big difference for those professionals aiming to succeed during hard economic times.

Using social media allows professionals to highlight what they do, meet with influential people, and create a profile that attracts hiring managers. Selecting the right content and paying attention to your online audience helps individuals create a strong online image that represents their experience and standards. Ordinary users need to understand how best to interact on LinkedIn, Twitter, and Instagram, as all three differ in their uses.

On LinkedIn, people create an online profile that shows off their career highlights and lets them connect with colleagues in the same sector. An updated profile with a good headline and summary will help users draw attention from recruiters and possible employers. Also, taking part in LinkedIn groups and joining conversations helps show that a person is seen as an expert in their area.

In contrast, Twitter is great for following what's happening in the industry and taking part in its discussions. Using popular hashtags, interacting with tweets, and discussing recent trends help professionals be noticed in the industry. Because it moves so quickly, this platform is best for those wanting to follow news in their industry and network with thought leaders.

Although Instagram has a personal reputation, it is useful for professionals in creative industries to use for branding their work. Using visually interesting content to showcase what they do, what they've achieved, or their regular work activities can make a portfolio that grabs followers' and clients' attention.

Building an effective plan on social media helps you make the most of these platforms. You should set up a schedule for your posts so that you don't miss any dates, allowing your followers to stay interested. Part of it is creating messaging that reflects what you want to represent in your field and life. Interacting with your audience via comments and messages can help you create better relationships and reach a larger group.

In addition, people can use social media to find jobs. You can find lots of job openings on LinkedIn, and tracking the right companies on this platform can keep you informed about possible job openings. You can support these organizations by liking and commenting on what they post on social media.

In short, social media gives individuals valuable opportunities to achieve a recession-proof career. Using LinkedIn, Twitter, and Instagram, people can improve their work profile, network with leaders, and discover new opportunities. In today's difficult job market, developing a careful social media plan that supports career ambitions makes it much easier to succeed and maintain progress in a person's career.

## Optimizing LinkedIn Profiles

If you want to increase your professional standing and find more career opportunities, LinkedIn is very important. Your online presence is vital in establishing a brand because it tells your story and shows what you know and what you strive for. A compelling and professional online profile on LinkedIn can be created by pointing out certain important elements.

The headline and summary are two of the most important parts of your LinkedIn profile. An effective headline should highlight your skills and what you can do for a company so people reading it take notice. It isn't only meant for job titles; it should point out your larger contributions to your role. It should go further than the headline by outlining your key strengths, what you have achieved, and what you plan to do in the future. You can tell your followers about your business by making it fun and informative at the same time.

Ensuring your skills and working endorsements are present in your profile is also very important. Your skills section should cover both your expertise now and the things you are interested in. Showing that others who work in your field trust you give potential employers a reason to believe in you, too. Better job results can follow if you include recommendations from prior colleagues or managers. A personal reference from someone you know gives a unique background to the way you present yourself professionally.

Many different LinkedIn tools are useful for developing your brand. One good strategy to demonstrate your knowledge is to publish valuable articles. Regularly writing about what's happening in your field or what you've learned from it can make you an authority in your area. Being a member of LinkedIn Groups that match your industry can build your network and raise your profile. Interacting with other people, exchanging ideas, and linking with colleagues in these groups can lead to exciting possibilities for collaboration.

It's important to have a LinkedIn profile that looks good and is easy to follow. Your initial impression of the platform will benefit from a nice professional picture and a custom background. Colors, fonts, and images in your profile should be the same as those used for your brand.

Finally, being involved on LinkedIn leads to a more interesting and lively profile. Updating your profile each time you finish a project, earn a new qualification, or achieve something is important. When you like, comment, and share your community's posts, you will stay visible and connected with those around you.

All in all, you should make sure your LinkedIn profile communicates your professional experience and that you actively join in on industry discussions. Working on these areas allows you to make your LinkedIn page represent both your skills and what you want to achieve in your job.

## Showcasing Expertise Through Content

Because our digital footprint shapes our reputation today, creating good content is essential for career success. It isn't just about creating material; it's about being recognized as an expert in your field. Using writing, pictures, and sound in their portfolio, people can describe their capabilities effectively.

Expertise can be established powerfully by writing. They help readers discover useful information and answers to problems facing professionals in different fields. Using this type of content, individuals can show how much they understand and how well they can think about topics, giving them authority in their field. Written content is also ideal because it lasts and can be used and shared with others.

Along with sharing information in writing, offering webinars and workshops lets companies engagingly share knowledge. Such sessions invite participation from audiences and encourage people to collaborate. When people offer real-world answers to challenges and solve them with innovation, they improve their reputation as people who find solutions. At such gatherings, people can react live, making the speaker seem both believable and easy to approach.

There is a strong need to pick suitable content topics that suit your audience and promote your brand. It means finding out which challenges and topics are most common in the industry. If creators work on these issues, their audience will be more likely to pay attention. It is important to select subjects that represent what makes you unique so your brand looks genuine.

Using different types of content formats can strongly affect how knowledgeable you appear. People are turning to video tutorials and podcasts since they give difficult information in an easy-to-follow way. They help more students by supporting various ways people like to learn. Additionally, putting together infographics and slide decks is a pleasing way to emphasize the main information and data.

Good content creators realize that consistency and quality matter a lot. Making good videos often helps the creator build a following and reminds them of their commitment to their area of work. Frequent and insightful advice allows professionals to hold their audience's interest and gain their trust.

It is easy to see that content can aid people in building their professional reputations. A podcast series on the market and investments is a way for a financial advisor to build trust among listeners. In the same vein, someone who knows what they are doing in technology can gain recognition by making YouTube videos that share information about new technologies and teach people their skills.

Publishing expert advice works for more than just informing others; it also helps create a brand that represents who you are as a person. If done smartly, publishing content helps professionals stand out and get access to exciting opportunities and networks. This technique provides individual benefits and adds to the overall progress being made in the industry.

# Chapter 5: Navigating the Job Search Process

## Tailoring Resumes for Industries

A well-made resume matters more than ever as people compete for jobs in a constantly changing market. Because every industry has its own set of standards, you need to create a resume that works well for that field. First, look carefully at job announcements to find out the main skills and experience necessary for the job. Adjusting a resume to match the requirements of a specific industry can greatly increase a job seeker's chance of standing out.

Customizing your resume is very important to its success. This often requires you to both use suitable examples from your past and make certain the industry-related vocabulary you use is accurate. Individuals should learn the industry's vocabulary and trends by looking at reports, joining networks, and finding job posts. When applicants insert these elements in their resume, they show they are familiar with the field and, therefore, seem credible.

Underlining the right experience is extremely important. When applying, emphasize education and experience that will relate to what the business needs. You should include work that matches the main responsibilities and use hard statistics or results to make your impact clear. Candidates should explain the actions they took and the outcomes they achieved rather than only writing their tasks since employers focus on increases in sales and improved efficiency.

Keywords greatly influence how well your resume is optimized, given that ATS is commonly used in today's job search. These systems scan the text of resumes to pick out keywords that are in the job description, which means anyone applying should mention these keywords naturally. Besides helping you pass the initial qualifications; it also ensures that the resume is suitable for managers who understand the industry's terminology.

Besides, selecting the right format for the resume means following common industry standards. If an industry needs consistency in work background, a chronological format is preferred, but for positions that stress skills more than experience, a functional format is recommended. If you learn about these small points, your resume could have a better effect on potential employers.

In essence, the goal is to produce a resume that checks all the job's technical boxes and demonstrates what makes the person unique. Each resume must ensure the writer is both credible and individual since it should stick to industry standards and appeal to hiring managers as well. If job seekers update their resumes to match industry standards, they will appear ready to deal with the problems and chances the industry offers.

## Developing Compelling Cover Letters

It is through a cover letter that candidates can introduce themselves and confirm their fit for a specific company. With a resume, you just put facts ahead of you, whereas a cover letter gives you the space to explain your eager interest in the company and your understanding of its goals.

Crafting a good cover letter should start with a well-written introduction that grabs a reader's attention from the very start. It is possible to mention a recent thing the company has done or admire the reason for its existence. Taking this route proves the applicant cares and helps tell their story in a way that reflects what the company wishes to achieve.

It's important to go over your most valuable experiences and skills as the letter continues. It's important that this section gives extra details and explains the resume, and it shouldn't restate information found elsewhere in the resume. If a candidate says they are good at leading teams, they might explain an occasion when they guided a group project to have important results or new ideas. It allows us to see better both their skills and the value they might bring to the company.

A great cover letter is built on personalization. Referring to particular company activities or principles that fit the applicant can build a relationship. It's also good to highlight if someone you know at the company has introduced you since this can demonstrate that you have mutual trust and let the company know you are familiar with it.

Strong closing remarks can finish the cover letter just as effectively as good opening remarks. It should again show the applicant's interest in the company and the position and mention wanting to talk about their contribution to its success. Ending your application with a direct interest in talking about the position can leave a great final impression on the hiring manager.

Many successful cover letters describe why the candidate is right for the job. A candidate who is switching careers could talk about how what they did in their earlier job gives them skills that will be useful in the new one. Likewise, focusing on the applicant's strengths can greatly improve how the cover letter is received.

A thoughtfully written cover letter should be more than just add-on material; it is an advantage that can add great value to a job application. When candidates describe their success, their fit with the company's goals, and how excited they are, they can impress potential employers.

## Preparing for Virtual Interviews

Being aware of the little things that make virtual interviews unique is important for any candidate. With more campaigns happening digitally, candidates have to handle new situations to gain a positive impact. It can be hard to rapport on a screen because you miss the presence of the other person. As a result, attention should be paid to how well the video and sound quality support the candidate's ability to present themselves as professional and speak well.

Being skilled at the technical part of virtual interviews ensures you avoid issues during your interview. It is recommended to check everything works well in advance so the interview doesn't hit any technical snags. A good understanding of video conference software is just as important because it helps the candidate make the most of the time allotted for the interview.

A successful virtual interview requires you to present yourself confidently. It is important for anyone interviewing to look at the camera, not at the image, and to maintain eye contact as if they were having an in-person talk. It helps you develop a good relationship with the interviewer. As the internet can sometimes make small communication details unclear, being direct and to the point helps to express ideas clearly.

Organizing your answer to common virtual interview questions is very important. Those interviewing for remote work roles are likely to face questions about their previous experiences and how they deal with remote challenges, along with challenges from work scenarios. Answering practice interview questions helps build confidence and ensures job candidates explain their skills well.

Now that virtual interviews are a regular part of the hiring process, job seekers need to get used to this format. Those who pay attention to technical readiness, develop good communication skills, and spend time on interview questions will be prepared to succeed in any digital interview.

## Utilizing Job Search Platforms

With the fast-changing world of employment, using digital tools can greatly improve someone's chances of landing a job, particularly when economic circumstances are tough. Each platform supplies a huge number of job listings and tools to help users build an effective job search plan.

Those looking to work online consider LinkedIn to be one of the top choices due to its dual roles in networking and job seeking. With LinkedIn, users can create extensive profiles that display their abilities, experience, and the support they get from peers. This site is useful for meeting professionals in your field, joining related groups, and discussing topics that open doors to new job chances. The search for jobs is simple because you can use advanced filters to select what you're looking for in the industry and at a convenient location. Frequently joining and contributing to LinkedIn discussions allows users to be seen by possible employers and recruiters.

Indeed stands out as a popular website, thanks in part to having a huge listing of jobs in numerous industries and areas. It includes jobs posted by companies, displayed on common boards, and listed by staffing agencies, giving seekers a wide range of roles. Users can also use Indeed to review companies and see salary data to make a better decision about who to work for. When job alerts are set on Indeed, users will receive quick notices of new jobs that meet their requirements, making the search for a job easier.

Along with these platforms, Glassdoor supplies information on company environments by relying on employee input and detailed salary details. This platform is crucial for anyone seeking to learn about a company's work culture and to negotiate their pay successfully. Looking at views from current and past workers helps job seekers know more about the company, and that is important for selecting the right career path.

Job seekers will be more successful if they use a strategic method on these platforms. You should make resumes and cover letters that are suited to the demands of every job you apply for. Taking advantage of unique tools on LinkedIn and Indeed, such as endorsements and resume preparation, can help applications look more appealing to employers. Furthermore, creating goals like applying for a number of openings a week or talking to several employees or contacts every day makes it easier to stay dedicated and organized.

It is still important to network in your job search, and these platforms help connect you with people involved in hiring. Interacting in a useful way by leaving comments or sharing useful articles can help you form business relationships and catch potential employers' attention.

The best results with job search platforms come from taking the initiative and understanding how to use them. By using the offerings of each platform, those looking for work can find many opportunities and present themselves as top candidates in today's market. Connecting your network and finding specialized tools online can greatly improve your chances of remaining secure in any downturn.

## Exploring the Hidden Job Market

As job searching continues to change, the hidden job market offers a lot of possibilities that people may not see at first. People break the traditional job-search pattern in this area and communicate more personally and directly with the companies they want to work for. It's important in this part of the job market to recognize that networking, being at the right place at the right time, and initiative can create life-changing professional opportunities.

A lot of job openings in the hidden job market come from personal contacts. Most employers prefer using employees or contacts for vacancies to avoid the higher effort and expenses related to public job postings. Developing a good network should be important for anyone looking for work. Besides your network, it is important to make sure you maintain these professional links. Going to events in your industry, joining professional organizations, and interacting on online forums helps you find out about hidden job vacancies.

A proactive attitude is necessary when trying to find hidden job opportunities. You should make contact with companies that appear interesting and ask them about chances to work together, even when none are currently posted. Your pitch should show your skills and explain how they address the needs of the company. It helps you show drive and prove your passion for the organization, among others, when trying to get hired.

You can learn about hidden opportunities by participating in informational interviews. The interviews are meant to teach you about a company or industry rather than to land a job. They offer an opportunity to ask about the company's values, the latest trends in the industry, and possible job paths while making your excitement for the role known to them. Interviews for information often have a good impact on people, and they can open the door to referrals and recommendations.

Being in the hidden job market takes a lot of patience and persistence. It's not so much about quick gains but more about establishing yourself as a smart and connected person in your industry. It means you're always in contact with your network, keep making follow-ups, and monitor news in your field. Due to your continued effort, opportunities can turn up, sometimes unexpectedly.

Also, using technology makes it easier to reach the hidden job market. These platforms are important for meeting professionals, connecting with others in your industry, and joining groups for discussions. Adding an online presence through a blog or personal website demonstrates your abilities and can interest others in working with you.

Basically, navigating the hidden job market requires planning, being active, and being determined. You should get away from using the same job-hunting methods and start using more personal and direct strategies. By paying attention to people, being enterprising, and frequently being involved in the industry, people can find jobs that might not appear right away but are very special. Choosing this method can strengthen your job possibilities and also improve your connection to your chosen field, helping you build a more enjoyable career.

# Chapter 6: Avoiding Common Job Search Pitfalls

## Identifying Common Mistakes

While trying to find a job with strong recession resistance, many job applicants encounter various barriers that can result in typical errors. Often, these errors result from people wanting to move quickly and feel more secure, and they can make looking for a job much harder. It is very important to notice these drawbacks when looking for work since the economy can be volatile.

A frequently seen problem is that job applicants do not focus enough on their application. A lot of candidates find it easier to apply to multiple jobs than to think through whether they are actually qualified, which can be a mistake. However, using multiple application forms negatively affects the quality of each, and any mistakes that are made result in added time and money spent. Employers easily recognize when an application is dull and not specific to the position.

Often, people make the mistake of not adjusting their application documents to fit what the job requires. Much of the time, resumes without appropriate keywords and jargon are not examined by an actual person, thanks to software. Candidates should know that creating documents tailored to each job shows they have useful skills and experiences.

Missing out on the importance of networking is another important error. Most people trying to get jobs look only online without considering all the opportunities offered by referrals and relationships. Many people find out about jobs that are not officially announced through their professional relationships. Connecting with industry specialists, going to industry events, and conversing in interviews can open doors and offer insights you won't learn in a job listing.

Also, people who are job-seeking tend to neglect how helpful a good follow-up can be. If you don't thank someone after an interview or networking event, it may be seen as a sign that you aren't keen or professional. Following up shows a candidate that you are still interested and reminds employers they should consider them.

If you don't take breaks from your job search, it can be very tough and cause burnout. Not all job hunters find the right balance between their job search and taking care of themselves. It's important to choose goals that can be achieved, rest often, and include activities that help your mind and body. Having this balance keeps you motivated and strong, which is necessary for continuing your job search for a long time.

Forgetting to prepare for interviews in virtual places can make things go very wrong. People looking for a job should get to know the technology, make the session professional, and practice being asked common interview questions to look confident and qualified.

Simply avoiding these typical errors can boost your probability of landing a secure job in any economy. The best approach means putting more effort into what matters, staying personal with your customers, and keeping yourself sharp and motivated.

## Developing a Strategic Plan

A successful career growth plan is built by considering yourself as well as the external factors impacting your career path. At the outset, people check their skills, identify areas to improve, and think about their ambitions. Getting to know yourself in this phase ensures you can set Goals that you can achieve. Awareness of your talents and what you want to develop further allows you to map your job goals to what you like and want to do.

Following that, gaining insight into job trends and the industry is important. At times of economic uncertainty, it's important to look for stable and upward-moving industries. Quite often, the stability of healthcare, technology, and essential services industries in the past makes them safer bets for job seekers in difficult times. Doing so also helps people grow their talents to fit what companies are looking for now and in the future.

Every effective career plan begins with defined and strategic goals. The aims that organizations set should be specific, measurable, achievable, relevant, and set with a time limit (SMART). Having goals helps people plan their work lives, which brings them motivation and direction. Using this process, businesses can both accomplish their targets and change them when circumstances or personal development demand it.

A strong network is an important component of any strategy. Meeting other people in your industry often leads to finding unknown job openings and understanding how industry trends work. Memory support can be valuable during a career, and such advice can help students get the most out of their experience. Taking part in professional groups and events allows you to meet new people and learn about fresh opportunities in the industry.

Learning and developing your skills should always be part of your strategy for your career. As the world of work evolves, you need to learn new things all the time. New skills and knowledge can be learned from classes, online classes, or by studying, giving professionals an advantage in changing circumstances. Having this commitment allows you to both work in more jobs and consider new career paths.

Along with this, the ability to be flexible and strong will help anyone succeed in their career. A good strategic plan must focus on strategies for facing challenges, staying encouraged, and improving emotional intelligence. Such features help individuals face difficulties and grab any opportunities, no matter the challenges they meet.

After that, a strategic plan must be regularly assessed, and any necessary changes should be made. Because the process is dynamic, it makes sure career plans follow personal goals and job demands. Regularly reviewing their achievements and updating their plans helps individuals meet their career goals and spot new chances in the meantime.

To put things simply, doing well in your job means making detailed plans, constantly learning, and preparing yourself to accommodate changes. If individuals make clear goals, develop a strong network, and keep learning, they will be successful in their careers over the long run.

## Maintaining Persistence and Resilience

Whenever the economy is not doing well, being persistent and strong is crucial for finding work. The process is full of risks, exceptions, and disappointments, and such a path can make it easy to lose willpower and faith. But, overcoming issues and moving past disappointments is necessary to reach set career objectives.

Experiencing rejection several times has a psychological effect and may lower people's self-esteem. Because of how this feels, it is even harder to continue searching for a job enthusiastically. Feeling upset by rejection is normal, but it's important not to let those emotions take over your good judgment or change how you value yourself. Resilience is built through finding methods to help you remain productive, look forward to your strengths, and not think much about the challenges you overcome.

Resilience can be built by planning doable goals and sticking to a plan that helps you work steadily. You may want to decide on some hours every day for applying for jobs, networking, and learning additional skills. Reaching little goals keeps you going and helps you stay motivated.

Going over the reasons an application did not work out can make you grow. Using suggestions from interviews and applications can turn downs into new experiences. The active steps help both for future work and also encourage confidence, helping with coping during this process.

Supportive people in our lives make a difference in how strong and flexible we are. Talking to people in your field and your support network can offer valuable advice and encouragement. When you speak with others who are looking for jobs too, you can gain new thoughts and stay less alone. You can gain a lot from taking part in support groups and joining professional associations.

Besides, having strong emotional intelligence (EI) improves our resilience greatly. EI means being aware of your emotions and also of the feelings of those around you. For people with a high EQ, talking with others and collaborating can be simpler during job hunting. Being empathetic, writing down your ideas in a journal, and accepting advice can make these traits stronger in work and life in general.

Keep in mind that staying positive is very important. When you think of difficulties as ways to advance and improve, your search for a job will feel like an exciting time for improvement. Using a growth mindset allows you to change negative ideas and concentrate on achieving more and doing better.

In short, being steady and persistent means more than facing obstacles; it's about getting involved and learning from them so you grow stronger. When you have goals, look for assistance, and continue to gain new skills, it becomes easier to handle the pressures of job markets.

## Overcoming Job Search Challenges

Facing uncertainty in the job market feels hard, but recognizing the usual problems and organizing a strategy can really boost your job search process. A lot of job seekers find it tough to stay motivated after they keep getting turned down. Feeling discouraged from rejection can erode someone's sense of self-esteem, making them less likely to try for other jobs. One way to conquer this is to strengthen resilience and follow a routine that encourages success. Sticking to what you do well and what you've achieved encourages a good attitude.

Many students run into another issue by sending applications for all available jobs, resulting in less concentration and poorer application quality. Instead, making a job search strategy is more helpful. This calls for picking realistic deadlines, focusing on how applications are polished, and adjusting job applications to suit what the job asks for and how the company operates. Making applications in just the right field raises your chances of getting an interview and leads to roles you truly want.

Building your network is essential when trying to find a job. Positions in the hidden job market cannot usually be found online. To find them, you need a good network of work contacts. If you conduct informational interviews, participate in events in your industry, and join professional groups, you are more likely to discover opportunities that other methods might miss. Networking allows job seekers to understand what's happening in the industry and the company's values so they can improve their application.

Apart from networking, learning how to use job search platforms is really important. With tools provided by LinkedIn, indeed, and Glassdoor, looking for employment can be made much less stressful. Activating job alerts, making use of powerful search filters, and engaging on company web pages can help potential employers spot you. Using these platforms, you can gather reviews about a company and wage details, which helps with preparation for both job interviews and negotiations. Finding a job requires you to be persistent and strong. Managing stress and rejection in the right way is extremely important. Gaining advice and friendship from mentors and peers helps you maintain focus and motivates you. Do fees zyth Having emotional intelligence is very important when dealing with the job search. Knowing and handling your own emotions, as well as being able to sense others, can make your networking efforts more valuable. If you learn to be aware of yourself, notice how others are feeling, and build relationships, you can make your networking and interview experiences more effective. People seeking work can overcome these obstacles by using a planned and knowledgeable method and can still find good work even as the economy slows. Developing resilience, making useful connections, and making the most of the tools at your disposal will help you overcome the challenges of finding a job.

## Building Emotional Resilience

In career development, how well you deal with challenges and uncertainty depends a lot on your emotional resilience. It is very important for anyone, especially in times of a recession, to be able to overcome troubles, change with the times, and stay optimistic. Resilience doesn't come naturally, but it can be developed by using activities that help with emotional control and how one copes.

To be successful, you must pay attention to emotional intelligence during this process. Recognizing how you and others feel and being able to handle those feelings are the main ideas behind emotional intelligence. With a high degree of EI, people often improve how they communicate, handle conflicts, and decide what to do. Having these abilities helps employees get along better, share responsibilities, and cooperate under stressful situations.

Before building emotional resilience, it's important to build self-awareness. It requires a full grasp of the way emotions influence your thoughts and decisions. Keeping a journal and being mindful may help you become more aware of yourself. Thinking about my emotions and noticing when certain feelings appear helps me realize what sets me off and respond differently.

Social awareness means you observe what team members feel and how they relate to others. When you listen and take part in team discussions, you enhance your ability to understand different people's feelings. As a result, people work in teams more efficiently and become respectful of each other.

Besides, strengthening resilience involves finding methods to manage stress better. Job searching when the economy is bad tends to bring stress because the future looks uncertain, and finances can be stressful. Easy ways to decrease stress are to practice mindfulness, exercise regularly, and live a balanced life. They are important for mental well-being and can also improve overall wellness, encouraging individuals to start their job search with renewed energy.

It is very important to form a good support system for emotional resilience. Associating yourself with mentors, colleagues, and professional groups is good for both support and encouragement. They provide us with important understanding, motivation, and guidance on the way forward whenever we are struggling. Listening to and following the experiences of fellow students can give you motivation to carry on.

Besides, when goals are realistic and little achievements are recognized, motivation and strength increase. Setting goals guides people in what to do and encourages them to be motivated. Acknowledging even simple achievements in learning supports good work and makes children want to continue trying.

Resilience really comes from adapting well and keeping a good mindset when challenges appear. People can resist challenges at work and succeed in every job market by embracing emotional intelligence, dealing with stress, and getting help when needed. Learning these skills increases the chances of career advancement while also boosting your development and happiness early on.

## Chapter 7: Transitioning Between Industries

### Assessing Transferable Skills

Locating and assessing your transferable skills becomes essential when someone is changing careers since the economy can be unreliable. Because they are useful all over the job market, these skills help people become crucial assets when flexibility and adaptability are important. The first step in recognizing such skills is to carefully assess yourself and list your experiences, both at work and in life, to see what you excel at. It requires taking a look back at past responsibilities and what you have achieved to see which abilities come up most often and have played a key role in your achievements.

Skills that you can take with you, such as solving problems, communicating well, leading others, and using technology, often cut across different fields and job titles. For example, skills gained from problem-solving in customer service can be useful on projects since these skills are necessary parts of the project manager's job. Just like teaching, strong relationships in sales often depend on the same interpersonal skills someone learns in a teaching position.

Documenting your abilities is more effective when you create a skills inventory. This checklist groups all abilities by strength and how much they matter for new positions. With it, individuals can see what their skills are and how those skills fit with different industries. The association that comes out during this step can suggest new opportunities that weren't on your radar in the beginning.

Skill audits are useful when evaluating an organization. Such audits ask participants to take online tests or receive feedback from those they collaborate with. Such resources show a person's strengths and weaknesses, helping plan what areas to work on to become better.

It is very important to know how these skills are applied in different settings. Organizational skills developed as a project manager can be key in healthcare and technology fields, which require everyone to come together and coordinate many different tasks. Creative skills in marketing also come in handy in financial services, where innovation in market studies and dealing with clients matters a lot.

Expressing and illustrating these skills helps when you are moving to a new industry. Discussing both your background and what you hope to achieve helps potential employers see why your abilities matter in the job you're applying for. Specific skills can be displayed during the process by including them in your resume covering letter, and talking about them during an interview.

All in all, reviewing your transferable skills is more than looking at your skills; it also helps you create a resilient career that holds up during economic ups and downs. Knowing these skills can make anyone stand out in any job market as someone flexible and ready for various opportunities.

## Exploring Cross-Industry Opportunities

In a market that keeps changing, being able to move between different industries can really help. Because the economy is changing, it has become important to spot and use opportunities from various industries so you can keep your job during recessions. There is an increasing demand in successful industries, impacted little by economic challenges, for people with abilities useful to any business, making it easier for such people to find jobs elsewhere.

Understanding what's trending in recession-proof industries is the first important step in looking for opportunities. Many industries, such as renewable energy, healthcare, and technology, are being propelled forward by a combination of new ideas and needed updates. The effort to reduce climate change around the world is driving growth in renewable energy, creating a need for experts in sustainability and energy efficiency. As a result, technology is being used more everywhere, so people with tech skills must work together in different fields.

It is important to follow the latest news and needs in these expanding sectors when you want to succeed in them. To do this, one should review industry news, reports, and analyses frequently. Talking to people from different fields can give you useful advice and lead to many chances. By joining industry-specific meetings, training events, and multisector gatherings, individuals can better understand and notice their target industries.

Gaining industry information and knowledge is important to finding relevant external opportunities. You can try this by participating in events and training courses on the topics you care about. While learning takes place at these events, attendees also get the chance to network with leaders and people working in the same field. Connecting with colleagues from different fields opens people's minds and helps them discover careers that fit what they enjoy and do well.

Often, learning about personal success in cross-industry transitions can help us understand the process. Let's look at how a teacher changed from teaching without tech to using educational technology. Using what they learned in education and new tools, they created a place for themselves in a developing industry. An engineer can also enter data analytics, applying their problem-solving skills to work with and control extensive sets of data, adding support to businesses in many fields.

In the end, companies must approach cross-industry opportunities using a strategic plan. A well-defined action plan that lists personal objectives and goals can help people successfully move through career transitions. The plan should have time set aside for learning and practicing skills so people can prepare themselves in an informed way for changes in the job market. Self-directed learning and earning appropriate certifications are still important parts of this process.

Overall, being able to work in different sectors is now commonplace and necessary for enjoying a long, solid career. If someone learns new information, builds their network well, and keeps learning, they can handle jobs in different sectors and remain secure in their work during a recession.

## Developing a Transition Action Plan

Anyone wanting to shift their career, especially in difficult economic times, should create a clear transition action plan. The first step is deciding on goals and checkpoints that show people which path to take in their career change. You should first look closely at what you know and what you have done, making sure it fits with the needs of your new role or industry. Part of this is a careful listing of skills to spot what you do best and what you need to work on.

After completing the primary assessment, the next task is to create both immediate and future aims. Immediate actions you could take are to join courses or get important certificates for your new job. Long-term goals, by contrast, aim for important results like landing a job in your field or moving up to a certain career. Giving these goals a timeline is crucial, as it drives actions forward and makes it simpler to follow development.

Continuous learning is extremely important when you decide to change careers. Participating in ongoing learning improves your skills and marks you as committed to your own and your company's growth. Some examples of this are signing up for online classes, joining workshop events, or getting involved in industry seminars and learning your matters a lot, as it gives individuals a chance to explore new fields and catch up with recent industry happenings.

A strong transition plan should include periods for research and networking as well. To find opportunities and challenges in the industry, you must first get to know its key dynamics. Getting to know others in the industry helps a lot since it provides insight and helps you build useful relationships. A good way to grow your professional network is by visiting networking events, becoming part of professional associations, and spotting mentors.

A transition plan should always include financial planning as an important step. Changes in your career may result in changes to your income and the expenses linked to additional training. For this reason, it's vital to prepare for the extra costs and try to find extra ways to make money if required. Sometimes, earning money with freelancing tasks or part-time jobs supports the future career path you want.

Ongoing adaptation and openness to suggestions can support you successfully during the process. Adapting the plan when needed gives you a better chance of staying on course during the transition. Getting opinions from others can improve how you look at the matter.

In short, transition action planning needs to be handled attentively and requires smart planning. When you have set targets, keep learning, and adapt your strategies, you will find it easier to go through different career stages.

## Navigating Salary Adjustments

Transitioning to a new career usually means you have to adjust what you expect to earn. Moving from one area of work or industry to another can bring on new financial challenges as well as major changes. To prepare, you need to be aware of upcoming changes and have smart plans to keep your finances stable and enjoy your work for years.

Often, once you move into a different field, you have to accept your starting pay will drop. Even so, it can feel challenging since getting qualified for a different field is part of the process for most people making career changes. If you understand that your income decrease is likely to be temporary, it will be easier to set goals and manage your finances ahead. What matters is to understand that these transitions can help people advance in the future. When you pay attention to big steps and upgrading skills, a temporary lack of money becomes a positive factor for your future wealth.

A new industry calls for a specific strategy when you want to negotiate your compensation package. To avoid misunderstandings, you need to research what people in your industry are paid. With this understanding, people are able to point out to employers the skills they will bring to the table and demonstrate their contribution during negotiations. Furthermore, taking into account performance bonuses, stock options, or more days off can create a package that matches your job and life goals.

It is also very important to manage how we expect our finances to change as we adapt. It is important to make a budget that can handle some changes in your pay. For this reason, you could find ways to reduce what you spend or take on side jobs to help you finance the transition period. Taking action in financial planning can make adjusting to a fresh pay scale less stressful for people.

Salary negotiation experiences from real-world examples help you learn very effectively. Some professionals choose to request extra benefits instead of asking for a raise, and others negotiate a signing bonus to reduce their first pay cut. They demonstrate how it helps to create unique strategies and build on your strengths and available opportunities.

When it comes to changing your salary, being confident is very important. Having confidence in your abilities can make a major difference during talks about your salary. If you say nice things to yourself, set reachable goals, and recall what you've achieved before, your confidence will increase. Getting help and encouragement from those with more experience can help you feel secure during the learning experience.

Salary adjustments, in reality, involve various steps, skillful negotiations, and mental strength. People who pay attention to their future finances and actively manage money can smoothly start in new jobs and continue to grow and be satisfied in their work.

## Building Confidence for Career Pivots

Confidence is one of the most important things shaping how well a person does in their career change. It is important to trust in your skills when moving into a field you haven't worked in before. How people view their strengths and how much they trust their skills affects their performance at work—being self-confident benefits relationships inside and outside the workplace.

To grow self-confidence during changes in your career, speak positively to yourself inside. Statements you make to yourself, and words to encourage can greatly change your attitude and make you feel more secure with new tasks. Achieving reasonable goals is an important way to grow your self-esteem. Reaching little goals over time can help someone believe more in their ability to be successful.

Self-doubt often comes with career changes, but that doesn't have to stop you. Remembering what you have accomplished is a way to defeat some of your insecurities. Understanding your achievements gives individuals the extra strength they need to succeed in future efforts. Besides, consulting with a mentor or peer can give you the confidence you need. Talking to those who have gone through the same experiences can bring you encouragement and helpful ideas to build your professional network.

Reading about confident career changers can show you how self-assurance can help you succeed. Notice the person who is not an extrovert but achieves success in leadership thanks to conviction and hard work or the athlete who draws on their toughness as an athlete in their office job. They demonstrate how confidence can help people power through difficult changes in life.

Mentorship is very important during times when you must adapt to your career. A mentor shares important knowledge that guides mentees in their new jobs. They advise you and also encourage you, keeping you motivated and accountable. Creating mentor relationships is a good way to boost your confidence since mentors can point out what you do well and help you figure out the best way to proceed in your new job.

When talking about career transitions, confidence involves both how you look at yourself and how you communicate with others. It requires showing potential employers what you're good at and what you can contribute. Having confidence when speaking with others can influence how others view your skills and how well you do during interviews and while networking.

Confidence for pivoting a career usually comes from thinking about personal achievements, planning for success, and receiving advice from others. It means working on practice and thinking positively to transform feeling doubtful about your abilities into feeling sure of your skills. When these strategies are followed, people can deal with changes in their work life boldly and discover many opportunities for a rewarding future.

# Make a Difference with Your Review

**The Job Search Guide for Recession-Proof Careers**

**Make a Difference with Your Review**

**Inspire Careers, Empower Futures**

*"It's not the strongest of the species that survive, nor the most intelligent, but the one most responsive to change." — Charles Darwin.*

A resilient career can protect you from uncertainty and open doors to lifelong opportunities. That's why I'm asking you for a small but powerful favor.

Would you help someone just like you, someone eager to build a recession-proof career but unsure where to begin?

My goal is to make finding, securing, and thriving in recession-proof careers simple, achievable, and empowering for everyone who needs it. But to reach more people, I need your help.

Most readers choose a book based on reviews. So, by writing just a few kind words, you could help someone take the first step toward a more stable and fulfilling future.

Your quick review could help:

- One more person gains career clarity.
- One more job seeker feels confident in their skills.
- One more career path has become secure.
- One more dream job turned into reality.

To make a difference, scan the QR code below or visit:
https://a.co/d/iCulJp5

If you enjoy helping others, you're my kind of person. Thank you so much for your support!

**JORDAN BLAKE**

# Chapter 8: Leveraging Mentorship and Support

## Finding and Building Mentor Relationships

A mentor's advice is very valuable as you face different stages of career development. You should first select potential mentors whose goals and values feel aligned with what you want to do in your career. In most cases, this work requires a strategic way to network with key professionals. When you connect with others in the profession, you find individuals who can teach you and show you the appropriate path to take.

When you approach someone who may be your mentor, it helps to mix professional behavior with true concern. You can show respect for their work and understanding of your background in a message that aims to let the reader understand your goals. Through informational interviews, an opportunity arises to familiarize yourself with the industry and decide if a relationship that could lead to mentoring is possible. To get the most from these interactions, have a real interest in learning and be ready for the mentor to tell you about their experiences.

After setting up a mentoring relationship, it should be carefully maintained. Keeping in touch and being ready to ask for advice allows couples to continue growing together. It helps to remember that in mentorship, showing appreciation and offering support when you can encourage you both to grow. It enhances mentorship and also makes the relationship between professionals closer.

Studying different ways mentorship occurs can help make the experience better for everyone. A formal mentorship structure with set objectives is available through employers, while people outside the organization may find their mentorships easier to personalize. Knowing what each model offers can help you match a mentorship to a person's requirements according to their stage in life and job.

The positive effects of having a mentor go past just career growth. At times of difficulty, mentors can support mentees and motivate them to respond more positively. They can give me insight into my industry, teach me about new possibilities, and help me discover more chances than usual. Also, mentors often help mentees improve their skills and abilities, providing the equipment needed for a lasting, successful career.

Stories are common that highlight how mentorship can truly transform someone's life. For example, a mentee whose mentor helped to join a different industry and use the mentor's advice to get used to the company culture. They highlight how having a good mentor can really change someone's career path by offering them both encouragement and solid advice.

Because the job market keeps evolving, the role of a mentor becomes especially important. With quick changes on the horizon for various industries, having a mentor to guide you makes things much more manageable. It is no longer simply wise to have mentors; in today's world, it is essential for anyone looking to remain successful after the current pandemic. Getting to a satisfying career is made easier by advice from experienced people and mentors leading us on the way.

## Engaging in Professional Communities

Being part of professional communities helps both your professional and personal development in your career. Whether found on the Internet or in person, these platforms give users great opportunities to network, learn, and move up in their careers. Being involved in such communities enables people to understand the latest industry developments, develop helpful relationships, and become more respected in their field.

Such communities consist of many people and are spread through industry-based forums, groups on social media, and formal professional associations. Every opportunity brings something different and encourages different ways of engagement. Joining either a LinkedIn group or a subreddit related to their trade allows workers to remain informed about what is going on in their industry. Participation is just as important as watching on these social networks. Thought leaders and valuable contributors often promote themselves by sharing wisdom, inquiring, and providing responses to challenges others encounter.

Professional communities bring more to the table than only information sharing. Being involved can open the door to real job opportunities. As an example, many communities have special job listings, group projects, and networking chances you won't find anywhere else. If you are known as someone who has useful knowledge and a helpful attitude, you may find yourself in the running for new work and cooperation. Besides, interacting with others can create the chance for mentorship, where experienced teams direct and support the careers of those in the initial stages.

The greatest results come from contributing value to the community. It requires both sharing what I've gone through and what I've learned and being attentive to the needs and questions of others. Providing solutions or suggestions when asked or simply answering other's queries is essential for motivating a shared sense of support and respect within your team or sector.

Examples can be found of professionals who have taken their careers to the next level by working with their communities. A content writer may find freelance projects when fellow members of a writers' group share information. The examples here point out that you can reach career breakthroughs and develop personally if you take part in industry communities.

In brief, professional communities involve more than just showing up at events or joining groups. You should seek to both collaborate and build relationships when your part of a team. During professionals' careers, these communities help a lot with learning, establishing relationships, and personal development. People who are mindful and honest can both progress in their careers and bring value to the knowledge and achievements of their field.

## Utilizing Mentorship in Transitions

Taking advice from a mentor becomes very helpful when dealing with career moves. A mentor's advice can greatly help people who are adjusting to new places or positions in their careers. A mentor shows you how to link what you already know to what you will need to know in your new job.

Mentors are involved for multiple reasons when employees move to a new role. They can give you advice about your industry that you might not find anywhere else. This same insight can help you learn about the culture in an organization, cope with politics, and find the unspoken rules that matter in the workplace. Anyone trying to adapt to a different industry or position where the routines are not the same needs to acquire this type of knowledge.

In addition to wise words, mentors motivate you and keep you accountable. Moving through transition can be challenging as it is filled with self-doubt and puzzles. Working with a mentor gives you someone to talk to and advice that encourages trust in yourself. Mentors will often set proper goals for mentees and press them to complete them, making sure all progress is slow but sure.

Developing a relationship with a mentor demands action and careful networking. People interested in learning should connect with mentors with many years of experience in their area of interest. You can accomplish this by joining relevant professional groups, meeting at industry events, and approaching people you know or meet on LinkedIn. Anyone who wants to be a mentee should show a real interest in learning from the person they are asking.

Mentorship can take several forms, and each approach offers something helpful to its participants. Having formal mentorship in the company gives employees a planned approach and access to things they need to learn faster. Those who receive informal mentorship due to networking get a customized and flexible experience. Starter packs can also be productive, as they connect people going through the same stages in life and who can swap ideas and advice.

Many stories illustrate that having a mentor can have a major effect on career changes. A mentee might be advised on how to use the skills they have to succeed in a different sector. As another example, a mentor might assist someone in an organization when a culture shifts so that they can smoothly adjust and maintain their productivity.

There are more benefits to mentorship than just career changes. They help form professional relationships that can continue to help and offer chances for progress in any business or school. People who have moved forward in their careers often become trusted by others, so they give back by guiding others and helping them learn.

Basically, a mentor can help turn a challenging job change into a smoother and more valuable process. When individuals reach out to seasoned professionals, they learn the skills and advice needed to become successful and prepared for any professional change.

## Developing Support Systems

Having strong support in place when facing tough economic times is a key part of career development. Both professional networks and personal connections give us stability and strength that influence our career achievements.

Support systems are important because they guide us, offer advice, and encourage us. Usually, this team consists of mentors, colleagues, people from the industry, friends, and family who help you gain different perspectives. Mentors are especially important because they guide their students, share what they have learned, and help with career changes. They can give you valuable tips for navigating a new area of work, which makes things easier when things change.

Strengthening professional links begins by reaching out to people whose goals are the same as yours. Networking events, professional organizations, or digital platforms meant for different industries can all make these connections. Getting involved in these communities helps you meet more people and find ways to cooperate and gain new knowledge. Being an active member of your field's groups promotes your career by helping your name become visible and giving you the chance to receive job referrals or partner with others.

Developing a support system depends equally on your links as well as your professional ones. At difficult times, such as applying for a new job, family and friends can support us with their emotions. They help workers feel supported and reassured, which reduces stress and keeps everyone's spirits up. Believing in oneself helps people overcome difficulties, encourages them to continue in their careers, and maintains their motivation.

Support systems might also consist of official and unofficial mentoring schemes. While formal development programs at organizations follow a set procedure, informal guides, often from similar peers, may be simpler to connect with and give more hands-on help. Mentorship in both forms provides different lessons and helps a person see all the options open to them in their career.

Developing a support system requires continuous attention and the support needed. If we provide and receive help, our partnerships with others become more robust. Trying to connect genuinely and help your colleagues be successful encourages trust and successful relationships in the long run.

Support from others actually strengthens your professional path and improves your personal growth. It gives us the chance to keep learning and adapting, which is important for success in the current work environment. Receiving help and advice from others encourages people to respond better to economic slowdowns. This is why having these kinds of systems in place is a vital part of having a career you are proud of, and that lasts.

## Real-World Mentorship Success Stories

Many find that being mentored is important in building a career since it provides direction beyond the usual job guidance. During a career shift, having a mentor helps people by giving them support and advice on handling the many twists of a new industry. Successful examples help us see the benefits of having a mentor and how that guidance can help someone achieve big improvements in their careers.

Picture a young person with a finance degree facing a decision to move into the growing technology field. She was guided by a tech industry veteran, who taught her practical things and helped her choose the right learning path. He would suggest certain online tutorials, direct me to useful projects, and sometimes introduce me to major innovators. Because of the personal mentoring, she moved easily into a tech profession, making use of her financial knowledge instead of seeing it as a barrier.

Once, a weary sales executive approached a human resources mentor, wanting guidance on beginning a career that wouldn't be so all about numbers. Because of his background in talent management, the mentor was able to give me important advice on gaining useful skills in my industry. With the help of her mentor, the executive received focused training and took part in hands-on projects, which improved her knowledge and confidence in HR. Her ability to succeed in human resources proved that the strategic help she got helped link her strengths to her objectives.

Having a mentor is also very important when dealing with culture shifts in a workplace, as someone new to leadership in another industry can see. The experienced leader guiding her gave her advice on understanding how the company worked and led teams in the new environment. With this mentorship, she gained what she needed to fit in and stand out, which resulted in a successful shift to leadership in the company.

They show how mentors are important during career changes, offering more than job advice by offering support, encouraging their mentees, and helping set goals. Mentorship can have a real impact, whether it comes through planned programs or just through talking to people you network with. With this mindset, they look beyond their current problems and can believe that what they want out of their careers is both possible and not far away.

The examples show that mentorship differs for every person since it ought to fit the different needs and ambitions of every mentee. Keeping a friendly atmosphere where anyone can ask questions and develop, mentors assist in understanding the road to a new job. As a result, they make opportunities real and show their mentees how to build successful and flexible careers, whatever the job market is like. They show how important mentorship can be for anyone reaching for their career ambitions.

# Chapter 9: Preparing for the Future of Work

## Embracing Remote Work

A major shift in job patterns has happened, with remote work capturing the most attention. The changes are lasting and provide a mix of benefits and challenges, not a temporary solution to today's global challenges. The main reason remote work is appealing is because it offers a great level of flexibility that lets individuals manage their jobs and personal time more evenly. Now, employees can work from anywhere, providing employers with access to a more diverse talent pool and giving workers many more work possibilities.

A comfortable and productive remote workspace helps employees a lot. A good office is more than furniture; it also includes a space with focused designs to help you remain efficient. To get work done in a remote office, you need ergonomic furniture, a reliable internet connection, and the best technology. It supports your everyday duties and also helps you stay fit by giving you less stress and fatigue.

Many now choose digital nomadism as a way to show it is possible and acceptable to work remotely. This way of life means people can have work trips while also enjoying new experiences. Still, it requires careful planning since individuals must be online all the time and find ways to stay productive in different places. Because digital nomads move from one country to another, they have to be flexible and plan their days well.

Different and individual strategies for remote work usually require a combination of planned routines and flexible ways to manage tasks. Those who do well working in remote environments often use time management, emphasize what must be done first, and choose tools that increase team communication and collaboration. They are necessary to avoid burnout and keep productivity going over the long term.

Being apart from each other can create special challenges for maintaining the connection and communication of a team. When offices aren't physically present, teams have to use digital apps more to help with collaboration and bonding. Keeping in touch by video, following clear guidelines for exchanging messages, and sharing files help teams despite their being far apart.

The increase in remote work has a major effect on how people create and follow career paths. It makes managers care more about what gets done than about seeing their employees in the office. With this move, employees feel happier and learn new skills since they have a bigger say in how their job is done. Even so, it takes more driving power and responsibility.

To sum up, accepting remote work means learning about and fitting into a new set of routines. It means creating a good work setup, practicing digital communication skills, and coming up with plans for bettering oneself and one's career. As remote work expands, it gives individuals a way to satisfy their career goals while enjoying life at home. Nowadays, being capable of working remotely matters in many jobs, helping people handle changing economic situations.

## Focusing on Emerging Technologies

As traditional jobs become threatened by ups and downs in the economy, new technologies are becoming sources of lasting opportunity and security. They are transforming many industries and opening up fresh paths for people to build their careers. These areas are led by artificial intelligence (AI), machine learning, blockchain, and data analytics, giving unique opportunities to everyone open to changing and evolving.

Today, artificial intelligence and machine learning are likely the most important advances in technology. Automation is applied to basic tasks and also to advanced functions in different industry areas. For example, healthcare companies are using AI to look ahead and predict patients' health outcomes as well as improve how they operate. In finance, machine learning methods support both fraud detection and assessing risks. To keep up with their advancements, these technologies need workers who understand programming, analyze data, and make algorithms, which creates many new positions like those of AI specialists and data scientists.

Although created to handle cryptocurrencies, blockchain technology is now being applied in many other areas. Being able to securely, transparently, and decentralize records gives it immense value in supply chain management, finance, and public administration. With businesses aiming to use blockchain to improve security and openness, there is now a higher demand for people who develop and consult on blockchain technology.

In almost every industry, data analytics influences and improves how decisions are made. Today, people who can work with difficult data and find helpful results are highly valued. Companies in marketing and product development use data analytics to analyze consumers, optimize how things are done, and predict future trends. Because of this development, people with skills in data science, statistics, and business intelligence have new opportunities.

If these technologies are truly integrated, businesses must shift their strategies and use new equipment. In healthcare, the introduction of telemedicine and digital health records is changing how people get and use their medical services. Fintech is also changing how financial institutions work, providing consumers with new options that are designed especially for them.

Professionals need to comprehend and accept these recent developments to secure their professions in the future. Getting tech skills from online learning, workshops, and hands-on experience can make getting a job much easier. Being aware of what's happening in your industry helps you notice new opportunities and adjust your career to fit the market.

In short, looking at emerging technologies helps you cope with career changes and also makes you part of new advancements. With the ongoing development of these technologies, many new jobs will appear, and old jobs will be transformed, making for an exciting time for those who like to adapt.

## Anticipating Industry Trends

Trying to foresee the next trends in industries is a key skill for anyone who wants a successful and safe career future. If someone masters this skill, they are ready to make the most of new chances, and their careers are protected from changes in the economy. It is important to truly observe what happens in an industry and actively learn how to adapt to continue growing.

First, you should be watching the latest developments in various industries. You can do this by joining industry newsletter lists, going to conferences, and attending seminars about the future of work. These websites deliver key information about new trends and changes happening in different industries. Utilizing these resources gives people the details they require to predict possible career advantages and downsides.

Reviewing trend data is important for spotting the first signs of changes in an industry. This means studying data and reports to find out which direction industries are taking. Using data visualization software helps analysts make sense of a lot of data, giving them conclusions to work with. When individuals recognize these patterns, they can take steps in their careers that are valuable for the future.

Society's changes have a huge effect on what happens in industry. Because people are choosing more sustainable and fair products, businesses need to change their approach as well. This is reflected in the rise in interest in using green technologies and following sustainable business traditions. Professionals who notice these ongoing shifts may use them to their benefit, becoming known as leaders in areas that support sustainability and ethics.

Besides, successful sectors prove their strength and creativity by adjusting to new trends in the industry. For example, the automotive industry's switch to electric and autonomous cars illustrates how mainstream industries respond to new demands. In the same way, retail is now using augmented reality to improve the shopping process and show how industries can respond to innovative changes.

During these changes, people are expected to develop a way of thinking that promotes lifelong learning and makes them more flexible. This means learning new things to stay up to date with the latest job trends. Staying up-to-date requires online courses, workshops, and other professional development events to keep the skills the industry wants.

In essence, watching industry trends is about both guessing what will happen and being ready for it. Professionals who are aware, study statistics, and understand social changes can develop the best strategies for success. Using this approach protects your career and helps you move ahead to new opportunities. Those who can foresee and adjust as industries grow will enjoy the most success when things are uncertain.

## Building Long-term Career Resilience

Being flexible and able to adapt through ups and downs in the economy is now key for everyone in the job market. Being resilient in their careers becomes important for people facing the uncertain aspects of their jobs. Being adaptable in your job is very important nowadays when the economy changes, and work roles and tasks shift.

Building a flexible career strategy helps by giving you different useful skills. One advantage here is that it expands your career choices and makes you better able to respond to changes in the industry. Designing a profound professional network is essential for help and upcoming career opportunities. Being part of this network can give you useful insights and introduce you to positions you didn't know about.

Being able to adapt helps people keep their jobs, making it clear that change should always be met as part of career progress. Those who continue to grow and learn to stay better matched with the needs of their industries. Taking this approach means having the expertise needed to handle the requirements of changing job duties.

A variety of examples show that resilient individuals adapt their careers when needed and continue to succeed. A financial advisor who shifted from their usual work to wealth management, thanks to their old abilities, could be used as an example. Moreover, educators might find success by using online learning methods, which are becoming increasingly popular.

Imagining your career goals in advance helps you remain strong through the years. Choosing ambitious and attainable goals for your career creates a guide for your plans. Seeing your career path in advance points you in the right direction and encourages you to keep going through obstacles.

Having a clear sense of where you are going is made possible by having a vision for your career. If a career vision is well established, it will steer your decisions to help you achieve your important objectives. Walking the talk by linking goals and daily work is critical, and this often means evaluating outcomes and making the necessary adjustments when things change.

Adapting in your career and moving forward professionally depends on keeping up with new learning experiences. Reading about your industry, taking online courses, and joining workshops are great ways to apply learning in real life.

Feeling curious about the world helps you to want to learn more for your whole life and love exploring everything you can. When people ask questions and become open to different ways of learning, they can grow a mindset that values discovery and new ideas.

Tales of successful lifelong learners serve as proof that always learning makes a difference in your career. Someone who advances their career in science through ongoing learning follows this principle in the same way as a business leader who stays at the front of their industry by updating their skills.

To finish, people looking to develop a stable work path should be open-minded, keep learning, and have a clear career vision. People who develop these traits can handle the difficulties and successes in their work lives.

## Creating a Vision for Your Career

For career development, deciding on your desired future is very important for accomplishing your career goals. Having this vision helps clear a direction when facing difficulties in career advancement. You need to start by setting challenging yet attainable goals for your journey. They act as markers, guiding the creation of a work path that fits your dreams and exists in the marketplace.

To see your way forward in a career, you need to reflect on yourself and think ahead. This means thinking ahead about what you want in your career and where you hope to end up. Knowledge of what talents, interests, and values are most important to an individual builds the solid foundation for a great career vision. Those who choose clear goals find it easier to follow the right path, as well as to keep motivated and dedicated.

Having a clear reason for your future in your career drives motivation. It serves to guide individuals in what direction to move and what objectives matter most. Being clear supports making good choices so that every action contributes to the overall aim. In addition, a solid vision makes one more flexible since it inspires people during hard times, enabling them to cope with problems more strongly.

To achieve your hopes, you must make sure your daily activities follow your vision. Sometimes, you review your progress and change your strategies depending on what is happening now. Using a flexible method, individuals ensure their everyday activities support their big-picture career plans. Having everything aligned means team members feel more committed and prouder of their progress as they reach their targets.

More examples of people having successful careers by planning their careers suggest the strength of having a clear vision early. Notice how a business owner's commitment to a mission leads to a flourishing startup or how a creative worker succeeds with clear and well-defined career steps. From what we see, making sure you have an established vision is essential since it offers direction to people working towards their dreams.

In brief, to design a career vision, you need to link who you are now with where you want to head in the future. It's all about creating a plan that you enjoy doing and that's reachable so your career meets both your career goals and what matters to you. When individuals act in line with what they have planned and what they want from their careers, they can turn their dreams into real success.

# Chapter 10: Cultivating Lifelong Learning Habits

## Importance of Continuous Learning

Because the job market keeps evolving, people need to adapt and grow now more than ever. Because the global economy keeps evolving, those working in it need to adapt quickly and see what is ahead. Since the job field changes rapidly, keeping up with new knowledge is crucial for anyone who wants to remain in the game.

Because technology advances so quickly, people and businesses need to keep learning all the time. Since automation and artificial intelligence are redefining many roles, gaining new skills is now essential for everyone. It's not enough to train on the newest tools; staff need to be ready to accept and adapt to advancements and progress. Learning throughout your career typically allows you to handle different roles and jobs with greater ease, which helps your career span stay long.

Further, gaining knowledge regularly encourages a person to evolve, better understand different fields, and think effectively through difficulties. Students need to learn like this, given that the market now values understanding across different fields and joining various concepts. Lifelong learning helps people build up a wide variety of skills that can benefit them on the job and in other parts of life.

It is possible to become a continuous learner by using different daily routines. You can learn new skills easily and whenever it suits you with online courses, workshops, and seminars. Being able to customize your studies this way makes it easier for professionals to achieve their career and industry aims. In addition, looking into industry publications and being part of professional groups can provide ideas on what's coming next and what chances exist.

Curiosity is very important as we learn these new skills. Curiosity helps people learn new things and also motivates them to think outside their usual areas of work. Learning more can lead people to surprising discoveries, and an atmosphere of creativity and adaptability is created. Professionals learn and create unique answers to tough problems when they explore different opinions and question themselves.

The success stories of lifelong learners show how learning throughout life can help in a career. An example is a researcher who keeps exploring new ideas and can make significant progress in their specialty and help form innovations. An awareness of industry developments gives a business leader the chance to make strategic moves that take their organization forward.

Basically, continuous learning helps you rise in your career and is also about seeing growth and change as essential. It allows people to succeed in the challenging world of work with confidence. Professionals who keep up with new learning opportunities can maintain a stable work life and handle both future and present shifts at work. Because of this positive approach, they maintain their usefulness to companies in any employment setting.

## Developing Learning Routines

To remain adaptable and grow in today's fast-changing workplace, forming smart learning habits is very important. During periods of economic worry, anyone looking for a successful career needs to keep learning and adjusting. Pursuing lifelong learning supports both personal and professional advancement while also guaranteeing that abilities are still usable in a quickly changing workforce.

Knowing the value of having a learning plan for your child helps you start one. Today's competitive industries urge professionals to learn new things frequently so they stay current with the latest trends and technologies. Learning in this way is about getting new skills and also having a mindset ready to accept and use innovation.

Start by finding periods in each day for education before trying to integrate learning into your actions. An example might include investing two or three hours a week in industry-related material, signing up for e-learning programs, or joining in-person events like workshops and seminars. It is important to keep learning on the calendar as a fixed priority each week. It means people can broaden their knowledge and keep up with what's happening in the industry.

Staying interested in learning depends a lot on our sense of curiosity. By being curious, individuals push themselves to explore more questions, find additional knowledge, and check out many viewpoints. It leads someone to study their interests further and find new abilities. Professionals who feed their curiosity often continue to learn over many years, which is vital for both their happiness and opportunities for advancement.

It's important to include learning in your habits away from traditional schooling as well. Succeeding in projects, helping out as a volunteer, or your performance in freelance work prepares you to make use of theoretical knowledge. Applying lessons directly to real tasks helps individuals better understand and get more practice.

Learning routines can be dramatically improved through technology. With online resources such as courses, webinars, podcasts, and virtual seminars, it is now simple to get a great education anywhere in the world. Thanks to these tools, students can choose their learning path depending on when and how they like to study.

Learning routines can be greatly improved by focusing on networking. Sometimes, talking with others in your profession or career can give you different perspectives you might not find through regular study. Through groups and online forums, participants can interact with each other, address certain problems, and receive suggestions for improvement.

Overall, having strong learning habits is key for anyone trying to create a career that survives economic downturns. To stay prepared for changes in their careers, people can sign up for more education, stay curious, use new tools, and take part in professional communities. Using this method, students develop the skills they need for today and for when new opportunities come their way.

## Role of Curiosity in Learning

When we are curious, we learn and develop a lot more easily. It leads us to try learning, knowing, and grasping different ideas and talents. When it comes to career growth, curiosity shapes people to keep adapting as changes happen in the job sector.

Basically, curiosity is what inspires us to learn. People learn to discover their questions and find answers, which allows them to understand their environment better. Having intrinsic motivation is what helps lifelong learners go past simply learning for current use. An interest in finding out more helps individuals learn by themselves, which is important for keeping up with today's changing industries.

Interest in learning encourages people to think in new and innovative ways. If individuals are eager to know more, they become more likely to generate creative answers to problems. Not only does this way of thinking solve problems, but it can also inspire original ideas and progress that improve careers and the success of an organization. When you are curious about your job, you may find new ways and technologies that make your tasks more efficient and effective.

Additionally, curiosity allows us to adjust better to change. Since businesses are always impacted by technology and the economy, adjusting is extremely important. Those who are curious about their field can respond well to changes in the job market and manage the uncertainty better. Since they are open to learning and changing roles, they are extremely important to their organizations.

Curiosity encourages people in teams to work together more effectively. People who are interested in learning often welcome different ways of thinking. As a result, people on the team are more willing to listen and work together. If people are open to each other, the team can function more effectively, and the workplace will be friendlier.

Additionally, having curiosity drives up the level of satisfaction a person gets at work. If people are keen to learn about their job, they usually find it more fulfilling. Motivation from within can make someone feel more fulfilled and vital in their career and may even help them remain at the job for many years.

Being interested in different subjects supports a positive attitude about learning, which helps you succeed later in your career. Someone with a growth mindset believes that steady and disciplined work makes abilities and intelligence grow. Anyone curious tends to see difficulties as motivations for growth instead of as hurdles.

We can conclude that being curious is absolutely vital for our education and our work life. It gives a push to learning all our lives and supports being original, flexible, working well with others, and sharing ideas. People who develop a curious mind often become successful, grow professionally, and help their organizations succeed.

## Lifelong Learning Success Stories

Lifelong learning is most clearly seen in the lives of those who changed their professions by constantly learning and adjusting. Not only do these stories move others, but they also provide helpful guidance for people trying to keep their careers safe from economic risks.

Remember how a seasoned financial advisor realized that the economy would soon affect financial matters? Rather than fighting against the trend, they decided to gain new knowledge in wealth management. Through additional learning and certificates, they were able to take on a job that fit their abilities and also took advantage of growing job opportunities in the field. Thanks to this proactive spirit, they retained their reputation and became a top name in the growing financial area.

In still another demonstration, one teacher was forced to get used to teaching online after schools switched from traditional classrooms. To face the change, this educator participated in workshops designed to teach digital technology and online education. Because of this, they smoothly updated their teaching and made their knowledge available to international viewers. Leveraging technology helped them sustain their profession and enhance the way many students learned.

An insatiable curiosity made a scientist continue exploring new ideas in additional subjects. They learned about the latest developments in their field by joining industry conferences and teaming up with experts from other areas. Thanks to their ongoing quest for new knowledge, they wrote major works in their profession, became well-known, and saw their careers go in surprising but beneficial paths.

As a result, the business leader also understood the benefits of being aware of changes in their sector and learning new things every day. Attending executive education and spending time with industry think tanks gave them a reason to stay ahead.

As they became more skilled, they also built an environment of innovation that benefited their company's performance and endurance.

They show that continuous learning is necessary to become successful in your career. They explain that committing to keep learning, officially or by themselves, can lead to new opportunities at work. Additionally, such experiences prove that adjusting to new situations and learning can help individuals find opportunities in problems.

Because the world of work keeps changing, these stories remind us that never stopping to learn is important. They demonstrate that one main part of resilience on the job is keeping a positive attitude and constantly seeking new ways to learn. The decision to keep learning, either academically or on your own, prepares a person to manage the many changes in the workplace.

## Incorporating Learning into Daily Life

Constant learning is essential as well as helpful in today's jobs, given how fast things change. By using this method, learning should become mixed into daily life and not remain a separate activity on a timetable. With this, people can make sure they are still important and up-to-date in their jobs when economic times are uncertain.

It is important to realize in the first place that many kinds of learning are always available. They take place somewhere other than in a classroom or training environment, chiefly online. Learning often happens in our everyday activities, such as reading the news and taking part in practical talks. Being aware that these are learning chances allows us to develop a habit of learning throughout life.

Using technology is a useful way to add learning to our usual activities. Now that there are so many online courses, webinars, and digital resources, learning has become very easy. Coursera and LinkedIn Learning give people courses on many professional topics that can be studied whenever someone wants, at their speed. Doing your lessons during your commute or lunch hour will make learning part of your regular schedule.

You can also encourage yourself to be interested in exploring new topics. When we are curious, we want to understand and explore, which results in natural learning. You can help this by talking, trying new activities, and having an open mind to what others think. Thinking creatively with other professionals, going to workshops, and learning about topics you are not familiar with can all build your knowledge base.

In addition, making your own learning goals can place your studies on the right track and give you extra motivation. The goals need to support what you want from your career, and they should be both hard to reach and possible to accomplish. If they have clear objectives, individuals know which skills and knowledge to learn to move forward in their careers. Keeping your career goals up to date benefits your learning and helps it keep up with new requirements in your job and industry.

Also, making your environment supportive is important to effective lifelong learning. You might do this by picking a good study spot, getting the tools or technology you need, and lowering your distractions. Joining a learning group gives you opportunities to receive both support and hold yourself responsible for studying. Being part of professional groups, forums, or study groups offers a way to learn with others and resolve tough problems.

Don't forget to honor and recognize the progress you achieve. Seeing how far you've come while learning encourages you to keep studying. Any course completed, mastery of a skill, or new insight into a topic should be celebrated since all contribute to your development in life and work.

Integrating learning into what they do day to day helps individuals stay up to date and grab new career chances. Taking this approach helps you overcome current challenges and learn to adapt to new uncertainties in the future. Making learning a habit each day guarantees that you'll keep improving and succeed, no matter what economic climate you are in.

# Chapter 11: Balancing Career and Personal Well-being

## Importance of Work-Life Balance

In our fast-moving society, the added stress of career success too often drowns out the need to keep work and personal life balanced. This state is important for both succeeding in your career and leading a happy life. Work-life balance covers more than just planning your time effectively; it includes mixing your career with your hopes and needs.

If you take good care of your work and your personal life, you are less likely to experience burnout caused by too much stress. Burnout can lead to health problems, lower productivity, and lessen creative thinking. Many duties at work can cause someone to be overloaded, which limits their creativity and makes it tough for them to accomplish tasks well. A balanced lifestyle helps people improve their work performance and keep their creative powers over a longer period.

Working towards a balance between work and life means putting health and well-being at the heart of your everyday habits. Setting aside stretching breaks, doing activities you like, and being mindful can all help you stay well every day. They help relax your mind and increase your feelings of confidence and fulfillment. Being mindful encourages people to concentrate and keeps anxiety down.

Besides, making sure our career plans fit with our principles helps guarantee that our jobs improve our overall life contentment. When your core values match your career direction, you can enjoy your work more. Distinguishing between your job and personal life helps you avoid problems caused by their mixing. If people define these limits, they can save their time and keep their jobs under control.

Good career success is more about both your achievements at work and your overall happiness than simply about your achievements. We see many examples of professionals who have made physical fitness a part of their daily schedule, which has helped them both at home and work. Managers who dedicate time to family as well as to their jobs prove that work can be done just as well if time is set for family.

Balancing work and life is aimed at making a lifestyle that promotes personal joy and work success. It is about making choices that demonstrate what you value so you do not skip on work or your personal life. If people find a good balance, their careers will be more fulfilling, and their personal lives will thrive as well. Thanks to this equilibrium, employees feel better and become more active, which brings benefits to organizations as a whole.

## Prioritizing Health and Well-being

As the job market can move fast and is sometimes unpredictable, it's very important for career success to keep oneself healthy. If you do not watch your balance between your job and personal time, attempting to achieve in your career can lead to exhaustion. Prioritizing professional ambitions is best done while making healthy habits part of your everyday life.

The first step to adding wellness to life is to understand the value of setting aside space for breaks and leisure. It helps reduce stress and raises productivity because it lets our minds and bodies take important breaks. If you pause for a break, activities such as walking, reading, or doing your favorite hobby can help lower the stress of job hunting.

Mindfulness, together with relaxation techniques, can help control your stress and help you stay attentive while searching for a job. Meditation, breathing exercises, or yoga can help you calm down, get your mind centered, and lower your anxiety. The use of these techniques helps our minds and also makes it easier for us to cope with the inevitable ups and downs of a career path.

Linking our work and life ambitions with our key values is a way to feel happier and better in life. If individuals connect their work to their basic values, they can find a happy mix between their job and personal life. Being aligned often helps people feel more satisfied at work and less likely to feel that their career isn't fulfilling them.

Making clear boundaries is necessary for keeping a balance between your job and your personal life. Doing this means setting specific schedule rules and making sure you have time for both work and personal life. With these rules in place, an individual can prevent job tasks from taking over their free time, which benefits both their mind and overall lifestyle.

Successful people who manage their time well give us hope that looking after health and wellness is very beneficial. People who practice sports and physical activities regularly often say they feel more energetic and can pay better attention at work. Executives who make family time part of their plans and ambitions show others that outstanding work results can be achieved along with caring for their personal lives.

All in all, when people use approaches that focus on well-being, they cope better and clearer during their job search. Following a wellness routine every day, with exercises, health care, and relaxation, is good for your mind, body, and your role at work. When connected to personal values and clear limits, your employment situation can support your health and peace of mind. Using this strategy for your career helps you continue to advance in your job while staying happy with what you do.

## Aligning Career with Personal Values

A rewarding career comes from doing work that is important to your personal beliefs. Matching assures both personal fulfillment and lasting results. At the center of this, identifying your core values guides your decision-making about your career. These values help individuals find the direction they need to fit into workplaces that reflect their thoughts and goals.

The first step in this alignment process is to assess yourself carefully. You must reflect on your values to figure out what is personally significant, such as being honest, using your talents, living in an environmentally friendly way, or helping the local community. Realizing these values leads people to find and take careers that fulfill their professional and personal needs.

Once the main values are set, the next step is to see how they fit with current job paths and what might be possible in the future. This process means checking if a person's current role or future job matches their values. Innovation seekers would probably enjoy a fast-growing industry, but people who aim for stability might find comfort in a traditional branch.

Creating boundaries in your work is necessary for your values and career to agree. Making clear boundaries helps people handle the balance between their job and personal time, stops them from getting overworked, and prevents their private values from being sacrificed for their jobs. For example, this could require talking about flexible hours, taking on assignments you are passionate about, or declining jobs that don't fit your principles.

Matching a career to personal values takes effort and must be done again and again. When people mature, their ideas and plans for work may change as well. Going over career and personal values once in a while helps to steer career decisions in the right direction as things change.

Considering your values when making work decisions raises both your commitment and feelings of job satisfaction. If people can see the value in what they do, they often become more involved, which results in greater achievements at their jobs. As a result, people not only enjoy their jobs but also benefit personally and receive greater satisfaction with life from their careers.

Also, when your career matches your values, you behave more truthfully in the workplace. By sticking to their values, people build real connections and build trust with the people they work with. They gain a positive reputation and also foster a workplace where everyone is valued, and developers are looked after.

A good example of career values versus personal values is a professional who chose to leave stressful corporate work to focus on environmental advocacy. Wanting to be more sustainable and help out, this person found happiness at work and understood how having similar values in the workplace can lead to complete success and happiness.

Overall, making your job fit with your values helps you understand and evolve as a person. While you need to spend time thinking about yourself, reviewing your choices, and making adjustments, the satisfaction from a truly rewarding job is definitely worth it. When people consider their values in their jobs, they are likely to feel happier and do well in both areas of life, career, and family.

## Examples of Balanced Success

True achievement in one's career comes from balancing what you want professionally with what you need personally. Look at how easy it was for a skilled employee to keep up with fitness while progressing through their career. Instead of being defeated by the pressure of a busy job, this person organized every day to work out since maintaining their health helps their mind function well. As a result, they grew more efficient at work, realizing along the way that being healthy matters as much as advancing in their careers.

And we can remember an executive who intentionally put family ahead of their busy work life. This leader kept their activities organized so that evenings at home could focus on family and emotional security. As a result, the executives were happier, and it also helped them at work, as being able to step away periodically allowed them to view problems with new and creative methods.

In some cases, achievement in the creative field has come from seeking success and also making sure their work reflects what they believe in. This person chose work they felt connected to so that their professional life expressed their principles. Because their actions were in harmony, they felt good about their work and also became respected, drawing similar-minded collaborators and customers.

Think, for instance, of a teacher who was open to digital technology, improving how they teach as the field of education changed. By introducing technology in their classes, they helped their students learn more and also increased their expertise, indicating that choosing to learn does good for you in any field. Because of this, I was secure at work as the market evolved, and I inspired others by demonstrating how being adaptable can help one succeed.

In these stories, we can see that having fun in daily life is equally important for success as achieving at work. In every situation, the heroes gained long-lasting satisfaction and success by combining their ambition and personal lives. As the boundary between work and home life becomes fuzzier, these cases help show how people can manage their careers and intentions. They prove that true success consists of living purposefully and happily, while work achievements match our happiness in our personal lives. Being this kind of project manager is essential for a lasting and successful field, as it prepares for whatever the economy brings.

## Strategies for Maintaining Balance

Because life is fast in the modern world, striking a good balance between a professional and personal life is growing in importance. When work and personal responsibilities continue with no rest, this can lead to extra stress and exhaustion easily. To find balance, you need to plan and work on aligning your dreams, work ambitions, and well-being.

A key part of balancing work and life is seeing the importance of working together instead of keeping them separate. It's about merging your personal and career responsibilities so that both are attended to. Good boundaries are needed to keep work time and personal time apart so that one does not cross over into the other. You could make sure your kids follow certain work schedules, have certain areas without gadgets, and arrange family bonding times, all of which promote harmony.

In addition, looking after your health and wellness is necessary for your ability to succeed in the long run. This means living in a way that benefits your physical and mental state by keeping active, eating well, and using calming strategies. It's very important to schedule breaks and recreational activities to avoid becoming burnt out. Taking pauses gives people time to get fresh and return to what they were doing, ready to give their best.

You can bring your life values and work goals closer together by thinking carefully about what's important to you. Being aware of your main values helps you pick a job that fits your beliefs and brings satisfaction to your life. As a result of this alignment, most people feel fulfilled and purposeful at work, which lowers the chance of disliking their jobs due to conflicts with personal beliefs.

Often, when stories about work-life balance are successful, they describe individuals who bring their interests into their daily jobs. For example, professionals might exercise during their breaks so they stay fit and deal with stress. An executive might make sure that professional goals don't take priority over time with family. They highlight that balancing one's mind and career is possible for many people.

It also helps you become strong enough to face the common obstacles and struggles you experience in your personal and work life. Developing resilience is about finding ways to handle setbacks and move forward toward achieving what you are going for. That means inviting input to improve and approaching new possibilities with a new outlook.

Maintaining balance must be done each day by checking and adjusting regularly. When life and work change, people need to change the ways they prioritize themselves. Being aware of what you need in your personal life and at work allows you to find the right way to keep work harmony. Because of this approach, individuals can work and live well in all areas of life.

# Chapter 12: Staying Motivated Through Setbacks

## Psychological Impact of Rejection

It can be very hard to succeed in the job market, especially in times of financial doubt. Getting rejected is one of the biggest difficulties in this process. Experiencing many rejections can seriously affect one's mood, motivation, and self-esteem. Having something you apply for rejected might cause you to lose confidence and cease seeking work. Dealing with repeated obstacles can make being positive and moving ahead a real challenge.

Being rejected can lead to a drop in a person's willpower. Rejection can be hard to bear and may discourage you from trying again, making it difficult to have enough energy to send job applications. As a result, people may feel too afraid to continue their job search efforts. When motivation goes down, fewer chances for change happen, making it likelier that someone remains out of work.

That is why having resilience is so crucial for children. A resilient mindset sees rejection not as a statement about not being good enough but as a way to get closer to success. You can reach this perspective by focusing more on what you do well than on what seems like failure to you. Recognizing and honoring each little victory allows someone to feel proud of themselves through good and bad times.

Adding a regular schedule to your life is a good way to face the effects of being rejected. A clear daily timetable gives people a feeling of structure and purpose, which supports keeping motivation even. Your regular activities should cover looking for work, learning new skills, and caring for yourself. If you find a balance between these areas, you can continue positive progress and stay away from the exhaustion that can result from searching for employment over a long period.

In addition, feedback from negative decisions can give you useful lessons for the next time you apply. Getting useful feedback shows what job seekers should correct, which helps them grow and increase their chances of getting a job. Always working to improve yourself keeps you relevant and proactive in your career.

Looking for new chances with a changed mindset is just as important. We have to look at every application with fresh energy and good thoughts, always considering it a fresh opportunity for us. If you view job hunting as a step forward with new knowledge, you can enjoy the experience.

Hearing tales of people being resilient and strong encourages us. A lot of people have achieved their dream jobs after facing lots of setbacks. These accounts help us understand that holding on and receiving rejection can actually bring us closer to our goals.

Job search rejection is common, but you can lessen its psychological effect by developing resilience. Adopting a schedule, recycling their positives, and sustaining a good mindset can help people cope with rejection and keep going toward their goals.

## Building Resilience Against Rejections

Facing challenges in the job market can be difficult emotionally, but this important part of what happens in a career is inevitable. Seeking to maintain motivation and a strong mindset as a job seeker, you need to understand the negative effects of rejection. If you are continually turned down, it is common to feel less confident and not want to carry on looking for work. Still, building resilience requires us to notice these feelings and figure out how to deal with them.

Keeping a steady schedule helps to deal with trouble caused by rejection. Setting aside daily time for working, improving oneself, and having fun makes life feel steadier and more productive. Having a routine, both keeps your life organized and helps you avoid feeling directionless.

Focusing on what you do well can help you fight the effects of being rejected. Remembering past accomplishments and the skills developed will make a job seeker feel valued and notice their abilities. The lessons provide evidence that a rejection is not a setback for everything you have accomplished or want to achieve.

Feedback from applications that didn't get accepted can guide you in improving yourself. Evaluating feedback tells people where they can better their applications and what adjustments to make to them. Taking a proactive approach means job seekers get better employment prospects and can see rejections as a way to improve themselves.

It is necessary to use a unique thought process after facing rejection. It means that you should be ready to check out new jobs or careers that weren't on your radar earlier. Being flexible in your skills can result in finding new options and expanding your possible careers.

Accounts of people overcoming obstacles are great motivators for people going through the job search process. Learning about others who kept trying and eventually succeeded can help job seekers not to give up. By telling these stories, we learn that holding on and believing rejection is a step forward gets us closer to our goals.

Having a healthy work-life balance plays a big role in resisting rejection. Balancing work and life allow job seekers to avoid burnout and continues to make them feel happy and healthy. Doing mindfulness exercises, working out, and participating in leisure activities can help improve your wellness and provide the energy to keep up with your job.

Building strength after rejections requires knowing yourself, making smart plans, and being positive about your abilities. Building these characteristics allows job seekers to keep going, considering rejection as a reason to do better and advance.

## Rebounding from Setbacks

Many see setbacks in the workplace as tough obstacles, yet they can greatly improve your ability to grow and be stronger. Having a clear path in any career is rare, and you should expect to face different obstacles at work. While these challenges are difficult, they give people the chance to reflect, make changes, and move their careers onto better paths.

When something goes wrong, it usually starts by making us upset, raising doubts about ourselves, and making us feel helpless. But you should view your emotions as a way to grow and better understand yourself. Thinking about the emotion's setbacks bring shows people where the obstacles to their advancement lie. Emotional intelligence requires you to notice your feelings, understand where they come from, and use them for positive action.

To come back from problems, it's useful to reflect on them. It calls for a detailed look at why the setback happened, spotting what can be improved, and taking results from these failures to shape future performance. This method helps us to develop our persona and also provides a better approach to facing challenges in the future.

Besides, people who possess a resilient attitude usually handle career issues more successfully. Being resilient means you can face challenges and also end up being more confident. Concentrating on your path to growth by practicing regularly hugely helps you as well. If they set practical goals and notice their progress, people develop confidence and don't give up.

Talking with guidance and knowing the right people can help you through the most difficult times. Being involved with a community helps an individual get new ideas, receive worthwhile advice, and motivates them with stories of others who have dealt with comparable issues. These connections inspire us and help us realize that facing challenges is typical in several fields of work.

If emotional and social approaches are not enough, you can also revise your abilities by learning new things. Continuously learning new things can help your career and make you more flexible in a world of constantly changing jobs. By being proactive, people are best placed to take advantage of new opportunities whenever they appear.

Strong determination and hard work are shown when someone comes back from setbacks. If you accept that failures are normal along the way, you can turn challenges into situations for progress. Looking at things from this angle helps individuals become tougher and support a rewarding and lasting career. Dealing with adversity, people must use their resilience and flexibility to prepare for future success in their work.

## Stories of Resilience and Perseverance

During hard times, people usually stand out with their courage and determination, showing us stories that lift our spirits. They share more than triumphs and also teach us important lessons about holding strong, which is crucial now in tough job markets.

One story I remember is that of a person who tried many different jobs but never gave up until they landed their dream one. Those rejections helped me grow and learn. The individual went over interviews, made changes to their approach, and improved their skills. They recognized that being persistent helps, so they made time to learn advanced technology and meet new people. Blinding determination helped them achieve a job that suited their aims and gave them a chance to grow further in their industry.

It's also inspiring when a business owner who did not succeed initially goes on to achieve success with their business. Facing obstacles with finance and the market, this entrepreneur did not give up. Thanks to their innovative business decisions, they made challenges a way to progress. Their story points out that it is necessary to change plans when situations change.

Moreover, these stories strongly emphasize the value of a positive attitude. Many who succeed in life choose to concentrate on what they do well rather than getting caught up in their challenges. Being motivated using this strategy also boosts self-confidence, which plays a big role in solving problems.

The emotions caused by rising rejections in life are difficult to overlook. Being unsure of oneself or doubtful is usual, yet those who surpass obstacles normally reach a point of mental toughness. Doing activities that promote working and looking after yourself can help keep you motivated. If you work on mental wellness, you could find that being stressed about job hunting is less of a problem.

These works stress the significance of having strong community networks. Talking to those who deal with similar issues can help you gain both emotions and useful advice. Building relationships with colleagues and respected individuals can help you find hidden opportunities and learn useful things about the job market.

All in all, accounts of resilience teach us that failures are a normal part of what we do, and we should keep going. They remind us that being focused, adaptable, and well-supported will help us face difficulties of any kind. Because of these narratives, we want to keep growing, understand what happens to us, and not give up hope no matter what issues appear.

## Maintaining Motivation

When it comes to a job search, especially when the economy is difficult, it can be very hard to stay motivated. About every cycle, people go through application interviews and sometimes lose out, quickly leading to feeling discouraged. Being committed to your aims is especially important if you wish to achieve your goals in the future.

Staying motivated is often made easier by creating goals that you can actually reach. When you divide the job search into smaller tasks, you'll have fewer stressful moments and more successes as you move forward. Setting objectives for your days or weeks will give you something to focus on and follow a structured path through the job market.

It's also important to learn positive thinking skills. Secretaries of State learn to see their challenges as opportunities for growth rather than as losing. Dealing with rejection can help you improve yourself and gain a better job in the end. When you think about each challenge as a way to get better and succeed, it helps your motivation.

Creating a network of people who support you is essential when working on staying motivated. Spending time with mentors, peers, or professional groups can help boost your spirits, guide you, and make you feel part of a community. Trying things together and talking about what you learned can push you forward and help you gain fresh knowledge in job searching. In addition, being part of networking or forum groups can introduce you to invisible job markets and chances that you might not know about at first.

It's important to control stress levels and save time for yourself as you search for a job. Regular exercise, being mindful, or taking up a hobby can both relieve stress and make you feel clearer. Engaging in these hobbies helps you step away from job-hunting and supports a good balance between work and your personal life.

Taking time to mark achievements can raise the team's spirits. Gaining an interview or getting a compliment on your resume tells you that you are making progress. This recognition can fire up your motivation and help you think about your skills and the chances for achievement.

Continuous learning of new things and updating your skills are important for your motivation. Participating in online courses or workshops is useful because it helps you improve professionally while also making you more involved in your work area. By educating yourself continuously, you find a reason and purpose, making sure you keep trying until you succeed.

In short, staying motivated when you look for work involves being organized, having a good attitude, having people who help you, and improving your wellness. Adding these ideas into your daily life can help you deal with work challenges successfully, achieving the outcomes you aim for.

# Chapter 13: Aligning Career Goals with Market Demands

## Goal Setting Based on Market Needs

In today's changing job market, making career goals match today's job openings is crucial to finding a career you enjoy, and that pays steadily. With this method, not only does one meet the job market requirements, but their skills and abilities also meet new trends in the economy and technology.

Before aligning your career with what job demand requires, you must first study the latest industry trends. People can choose appropriate career goals when they know which sectors and skills are important. Renewable energy, technology, and healthcare are regularly selected for their ability to adapt and increase growth potential. Working on these skills helps someone find stability and chances to move ahead in their field.

Making SMART career goals allows you to fit your aims with the job market. This way of working helps people plan wisely so each move they take is aligned with their big career aspirations. If data analysis is a rising trend, for instance, someone might want to accomplish a data analytics certification within six months and use those skills in related jobs.

Regular learning is an important part of meeting the necessary skills required in the job market. Because the job market is always changing, what you learn today may not be useful tomorrow. For this reason, committing to taking online courses, attending workshops, and joining in on professional development is necessary. By staying current with skills, individuals better themselves, which normally appeals to possible employers.

Talking with others in the industry helps you identify important trends and choose a suitable career path. Taking part in networking, online debates, and professional organizations allows you to learn about fresh trends and what's happening in the industry. Spending time on these interactions helps individuals find out the qualification's employers search for, improving their plans for a career.

Using methods to assess a career can also align a person's plans with what businesses need. They give you an understanding of your traits, areas of work you could improve on, and the types of jobs that match your personality. Understanding what you can do and what the market requires allows you to select the best path for your future.

Elevating your brand and receiving mentorship are final ways to aid you in progressing in alignment with your chosen market. A strong personal brand shares your talents with others, while mentors show you the way through career problems.

So, to succeed in this way, you should develop plans, keep updating your skills, and stay involved in what is happening in your industry. Those who work in emerging sectors stay relevant to employers, achieve happiness in their work, and protect their careers from any economic uncertainties.

## Importance of Lifelong Learning

Because things are always evolving at work, we have to keep learning continuously. When the workplace transforms with new technology, being adaptable helps keep your career going and gives you advantages. Never stopping to learn new things is required to keep up in your job and stay relevant in the industry.

Along the way, education helps link what has been done to what will come next in any profession. Professionals can keep up to date with new trends, technology, and creative ways of doing things with it. As people seek more understanding, they build the skills necessary to manage the many changes happening in workplaces today.

It is especially clear in swiftly evolving industries that learning all your life matters. For example, in the tech industry, programming languages and frameworks develop so fast that they are hard to follow. People in this industry are required to upgrade their know-how to stay useful constantly. Acquiring new skills is simple with online courses, workshops, and certificates so that your abilities stay relevant.

Furthermore, continuous learning helps you keep an interested and adventurous outlook. When people use this approach, they often discover they are more flexible and open to new ideas, which matter greatly in any job. Curious people want to explore new fields, ask questions, and hear other people's viewpoints. A problem-solving mind can result from being open, and this skill is needed in most jobs.

Gaining new knowledge isn't the only positive outcome of continuous learning. In addition, physical activity helps you grow personally by increasing your confidence and self-esteem. As we develop new skills and understanding, we usually feel proud of what we have accomplished. Such positive feedback encourages people to learn and advance and forms a good cycle of progress.

Learning occurs best when you purposely decide to do it daily with discipline. If you commit a small amount of time to reading or taking industry-related courses, you can easily connect learning with your day-to-day life. Podcasts and webinars are good ways to use time during your commute or lunch break to improve yourself.

You can find lots of individuals who have used continuous learning to do great things in their careers. For example, a scientist may improve their work by attending more courses, and a business leader may do so by paying attention to new industry trends. They demonstrate that education at any time of life can boost careers, always making a difference with ups or downs in the job market.

Basically, committing to lifelong study is a smart decision for your future. It strengthens one's ability at work and also prepares them for surprises and unexpected situations. By cultivating new skills, professionals become better able to deal with the challenges brought by changes in the world. As a result, constantly learning new things allows individuals to ensure their careers are safe from recessions and helps them react quickly to changes in job opportunities.

## Tools for Career Alignment

In order to secure a successful and stable career today, professionals need to follow the competitive demands of the job market. You must form a strategy by closely looking at trends in your industry, your abilities, and the tools you have available. Career assessment tools are an important part of career alignment. They direct individuals in making career decisions, showing what skills are important and which paths will match what the job market needs.

Platforms that assess careers have several tools, such as psychometric tests and assessments of personality, to help understand traits related to your career. Applying these tools properly allows individuals to choose industries that make the best use of their strengths and experience. With LinkedIn and Glassdoor, you don't just find work opportunities but also discover what's new in your industry and what is expected by different employers.

Another important way to fit career goals with what the market needs is by always improving your skills. Because online courses and webinars are so easily accessible, individuals can learn new skills any time they choose. Being flexible is very important because industry changes due to new technologies and approaches happen fast. Joining specific webinars and workshops for your industry can open doors to networking, letting you meet people who can suggest career paths and options.

Besides, following personal development strategies helps a lot with career alignment. One, for example, can use personal branding to help themselves come across well to possible employers. Crafting a story emphasizing one's skills helps one's professional image stay true to what target sectors look for. Having a mentor is very helpful because mentors can guide you individually, assist you through changes in your career, and ensure your goals are in line with industry trends.

Talking with and meeting people in your sector continues to be important for connections and discovering new opportunities. Being part of professional groups, online and offline, supports your reputation and lets you display your skills and talents. With LinkedIn, people can build connections, share ideas, and access tips and jobs from industry authorities.

You should always have clear and measurable aims for your career if you want your goals to be in line with the market. Here, you should start by understanding what is growing in different careers and then choose ambitious and realistic goals to follow. Assess the company's objectives to keep them up to date with the latest changes in market trends. Following new developments in the industry and seeking to improve their skills allows people to become important workers in their fields and face fluctuations in economic growth.

Put, career alignment is something you need to keep working on by using the right methods. Utilizing career testing websites, always learning, making a personal brand, and building strong professional relationships will help people stay in step with the job market and enjoy a long and successful career.

## Personal Development Strategies

Now that we live in a rapidly changing work environment, personal growth is key to building a career that can handle challenges in the economy. Focusing on personal development can help anyone align their working life with what is needed in the market and prosper when times are tough.

Creating a solid personal brand is a main tactic that helps. Years of experience and your accomplishments matter, but what matters most is telling how your experiences, skills, and values come together to help you succeed. If you want to maintain a good professional identity, your brand should always behave the same in person and online.

Being mentored is very important for improving yourself. Talking to people who understand the field and help can boost your career progress much faster. Having a mentor means they can guide you on challenges specific to your industry and can introduce you to networks that open up new possibilities. It starts with contacting professionals in your area and joining in on relevant events.

Adaptability and flexibility should be key goals in every company. Having the ability to deal with new positions and use advanced technology in workplaces matters a lot. It requires being open to adjusting, receiving useful feedback, and studying new ideas as they come up. When a professional can move with the industry's changes, they enjoy more stability in their career.

To adapt, you need communication, problem-solving, and emotional intelligence skills. They support group efforts, creative solutions to challenges, and successful ways to manage interactions in a workplace, which is why they are required everywhere. You can become proficient in these by listening attentively, collaborating with groups outside your department, and asking fellow employees and your mentor for input.

As emerging markets grow, it is necessary to enhance one's abilities. First, experts should find out what data analysis, digital marketing, and social media management involve. Looking closely at which skills need improvement and then listening to the feedback from others helps define the right steps for growing your abilities. Joining online courses and going to specialized workshops can help you fill in these gaps well.

Experience from practical work is as important. Volunteering or freelancing with what you've learned helps you remember more and adds to your professional accomplishments. Doing practical work with what you've learned both proves your skills and increases your trust in your abilities.

Using online learning tools can make a big difference in personal development. Coursera and LinkedIn Learning give learners many opportunities to learn about the latest developments and trends in the market. Taking courses that match what you want to do in the future, keeping a regular study routine, and staying involved in chats can make your learning experience better.

In reality, personal development strategies are intended to secure the foundation of your career. Having these abilities and learned strategies helps your professional identity resist the challenges that downturns can create.

## Examples of Effective Goal Setting

Having effective goals is very important when working on career planning and development. Many times, reaching success in a career involves having set goals to help people navigate the challenges of finding work. Keep in mind that to get what you want in your career, learning how to set effective goals is necessary, especially in challenging economic times.

Think about the individual who worked hard to be appointed to a leadership position within her company. The first step was setting small targets that would inspire her along her way to her main goal. All objectives were carefully developed based on the SMART method, which made sure each one was seen to be attainable. Having this structure allowed her to see where she stood and adjust where needed.

On another occasion, someone made a clear plan with specific goals, which allowed them to switch from one career path to a totally new one. The person understood that choosing realistic goals was important and picked a smart plan for switching careers. Getting the big goal into smaller, simpler tasks made it possible for him to add new skills and build useful connections in the field. Reaching each milestone encouraged him and helped him stay determined to finish the transition.

It is very important to look at milestones when monitoring the progress of development. Recognizing small steps helps you maintain your energy and keeps you going. Because of these holidays, people can review their long-term ambitions to check if they are still focused on their personal and work goals. Examining the process continuously allows the team to respond to fresh circumstances and maintain their main objective.

For example, effective goal-setting works exist not only for people but also for companies or organizations. In a lot of successful businesses, it encourages employees to link their objectives with the company's broader objectives. Because of this alignment, people often feel more connected and engaged, which increases their productivity. Besides, when companies focus on setting goals, they usually give employees access to resources and support needed to accomplish their objectives, which leads to a supportive work environment.

Setting goals effectively helps transform things you want to happen into real outcomes. Clear goals and understanding what to do to reach them help individuals take on job market difficulties with poise and confidence. Whether someone is seeking a leadership role, changing careers, or working toward career and organizational goals together, the principles of good goal setting help direct them on their career path.

# Chapter 14: Navigating Industry Disruptions and Opportunities

## Key Industry Disruptions

Currently, industries are changing dramatically because of technological progress, new rules, and consumers' changing preferences. Such disruptions are transforming work, which presents both roadblocks and opportunities for people in the workforce. When industries grow and develop, what people do in them and the skill sets needed also shift, requiring people to stay on top of these changes to have a secure work life.

Automation and artificial intelligence are among the top generators of these changes, mostly thanks to ongoing technological advancements. Because of this change, people who are used to operating machines are now providing AI development, servicing, and monitoring support. More and more demand for data scientists and analysts arises as businesses rely on machine learning in different fields.

Regulations greatly influence industry trends. As a result of new rules for transparency and consumer protection, the financial services sector regularly changes its practices. As a result, people in the industry may need to create new compliance jobs, and those already in the field should keep learning to follow new guidelines. As a result, companies in many sectors are implementing eco-friendly practices because of environmental regulations, which have increased activity and employment in renewable energy and support for sustainability.

The way people shop is also influencing changes within industries. People who care more about the environment are buying more sustainable products and services. The automotive industry is experiencing a major move toward electric vehicles. Due to the growing demand, businesses are investing a lot in electric and hybrid technology education for engineers and technicians.

Fintech demonstrates that people's taste for convenience and technology is changing many different industries. Online banking and digital payment methods are now used more than ever, so traditional banks are now working to keep up with newer fintech firms. With these changes coming to companies, more people with expertise in cybersecurity, software development, and digital marketing are necessary.

Since so much is changing, staying adaptable and proactive while planning your career is important. Participants in such a learning process must gain new skills and also notice and understand major developments that are affecting industry trends. We can navigate today's changes by working on our skills in popular occupations and aiming for goals that match current trends.

Simply understanding and foreseeing changes are the main factors in success during periods of journey. Being able to adapt to changes in the industry is necessary, not only helpful,

## Opportunities from Disruptions

In the world of career changes, disruptions help lead to new opportunities. No matter if the changes come from technology, new rules, or people's preferences, these changes redesign businesses and open doors for creativity and progress. As we see more automation in manufacturing, jobs in artificial intelligence and machine learning appear, too. Much like technology, rules or laws affecting financial services can individually cause new compliance careers to emerge and require new skills from employees.

Changes from these disruptions are not only about new job openings. There is a need for smile providers to rethink what they already do and learn new things. The progress of industries means the workforce has to grow and change, too. The ability to adapt is very important for professionals wanting to take advantage of these changes. Participating in learning and training gives people a head starts in handling changes in the job world.

The changes in how we work have made the gig economy an attractive route for people who prefer it to standard jobs. Because of freelance platforms, experts have a flexible way to apply their talents to various jobs, making it easier to earn a consistent income when things in the economy change. Even though there are a wide variety of gig work projects and people can choose their own time, they may not have a stable income. But if you build a good online portfolio and join gig websites, you'll have a consistent flow of work.

Disruptions apart from gig work led people to consider different directions for their careers. In this example, professionals are able to move into consulting work during periods when business operators make downsizing changes. This way of working gives people job security and helps them make good use of what they have learned.

In addition, disruptions often point out that running businesses sustainably is important to help grow areas such as renewable energy and sustainable growth. As organizations aim to follow environmental rules and answer the needs of customers, sustainability experts are often in great need. This change proves why matching individual ambitions with market needs is key to lasting success in anything you do.

When the industry is moving forward, networking and mentorship are very helpful. Because of mentors and industry leaders, individuals learn market trends and chances to improve their businesses. A good example is when a print journalist changes to making news content for the internet, demonstrating how people can adjust in response to change.

The most important thing for success in a rapidly changing job market is to accept change and keep learning. With a prepared mind and skills, professionals are able to navigate uncertain times and overcome challenges more easily. That is, challenges can open new doors and provide chances to redesign your career positively.

## Responding to Industry Changes

Because the economy is always changing, being able to change with the industry is now crucial. When industries advance, face new rules, or respond to different consumer behaviors, experts need to create ways to stay important and competitive. If we understand these changes and respond properly, we may find new doors and ensure our careers are safe for the future.

Industries are going through fast changes because of multiple influences. New technological creations are altering many parts of human work. Automation and artificial intelligence are playing a big role in changing manufacturing, finance, and retail. Because of this growing use of technology, we now need individuals with new skills, and we are also seeing the rise of AI specialists and digital transformation consultants. Professionals are required to stay informed about new technologies and improve their skills to address industry advances.

When regulations are updated, this can have a big impact on an industry's direction. All over the world, there are new regulations that limit business operations in the areas of the environment and data protection. As a result of these changes, workplaces must follow the rules and sometimes hire employees whose job is to track organizational compliance with the new rules. As a result, data privacy laws have increased the number of organizations needing compliance officers and cybersecurity experts. Valuable professionals in their companies are those who are proactive about adapting to new rules.

How consumers behave is a main influence on changes in the industry. Since customers are looking for sustainable and ethical products, companies have to make adjustments to what they provide. More people in the market for fashion and food want goods that are produced mindfully and without hurting the environment. Experts in these fields should adapt to sustainability, use their abilities to match changing demands, and be flexible.

People in the industry should continue improving their skills and knowledge to respond well to changes. If people in this industry grow their abilities and follow new industry developments, they can predict any changes and get ready accordingly. It's important to gain skills like computing and programming, as well as improve communication, adaptation, and problem-solving skills within the working environment to handle new changes.

Responding to changes in the industry greatly depends on networking. Forming connections both inside and outside of your field can give you helpful information about what is changing and what new possibilities arise. Being part of groups, going to relevant gatherings, and joining online communities can explain how the industry functions and help form partnerships that push your career forward.

Finally, professionals ought to develop a belief that embraces changes as a way to improve themselves. Interpreting change in the industry as an opportunity to try something new in your career can help you succeed. Anyone who remains active, flexible, and interested in new knowledge can manage new developments and drive progress in their subject.

## Adaptive Career Examples

To remain successful in today's job market, you should be adaptable. Because industries change as technology and the economy change, workers should learn how to pivot and go after new opportunities. Examples of people who have managed well with career changes are used to highlight adaptability as essential to building careers resistant to economic downturns.

As more traditional media companies closed, a veteran print journalist had to find a new way. Because digital content was becoming more popular, she decided to focus on creating it. As a result, she had to pick up skills in digital advertising and SEO, as well as find a new way to tell her stories on the internet. Being open to digital technology helped her admit to a new job and illustrated that having these skills is very valuable today.

In the same situation, a financial advisor who experienced uncertainty when the economy turned down decided to move into wealth management. Because he understood finance well and acquired skills with digital financial tools, he was able to offer his clients creative solutions and custom financial ideas. Adapting in this way helped his career, made him a major figure in his chosen area, and proved the importance of being flexible in business.

In education, a teacher who has experience welcomed digital changes by including technology in her teaching. Because institutions moved to online learning, she began using digital resources to support student learning and engagement. The fact that she always improved her abilities gave her an advantage as an educator, pointing out that being willing to change keeps you up to date with the latest demands in training.

How healthcare adapts to change is also quite impressive. After starting as a traditional nurse, she learned to handle telemedicine as well. Because of this change, she could continue helping her patients and meet the greater need for using virtual services. Being able to switch tasks not only kept her position but also made her better at her job and important in a fast-changing field.

Such situations prove how being adaptable helps people keep their careers. Adaptability matters since it helps people grow new skills, join developing industries, or change how they work in their current field. Professionals can cope with challenges and make real progress by learning more and being ready for change.

We see from these accounts that being adaptable is more than a strategy for living—it also gives people an edge. When professionals are flexible and active, they can link their careers with the needs of the market, making certain they stay useful and free from panic when conditions are uncertain. As our workplaces change, the power to adapt will continue to determine the future of strong careers that resist recessions.

## Aligning Goals with Market Demands

Because the job market changes so often, it is necessary to adjust your career plans to meet the current needs in order to succeed and stay ahead. You should begin by understanding what is happening in the market now and by looking ahead to see what will change. Those who can identify sectors that are increasing or that fare well through economic problems can choose careers that have both potential and reliability.

Before making your goals match with what the market needs, you need to do comprehensive market research. Part of this work is to look at industry reports, learn about the economy and its indicators, and keep track of new technological advances that could change job and skill needs. People can see where growth is happening in renewable energy, technology, and healthcare and strive to find positions in those sectors.

You should make sure your professional goals are set clearly and measurably. You should not aim only to get a job in tech but also to closely define your plans and goals, such as being a data analyst in a renewable energy company in the next two years. As a result, everyone understands what to do and how to get there. People can use this to help themselves get the important qualifications and experience that employers in their line of work are looking for.

Being willing to learn new things supports your ability to handle any changes in the market. Many industries change so quickly that things much sought after one day may not be required the next. Accordingly, taking online courses, joining workshops, and getting certificates are necessary. Joining online seminars and networking opportunities within the industry can show trends and the qualities that matter over the years ahead.

Networking is still a key method for attaching career goals to what is needed in the job market. Connecting with experts in the industry can give you an edge, revealing what the industry requires and showing you hidden job opportunities. Being active in online communities and forums gives people the chance to keep up with industry news and learn directly about the abilities employers are looking for.

There are many tools available to help you line up your career. With a career assessment platform, people can learn about their abilities and interests in relation to job openings, and mentorships can help answer questions about careers. Using these resources helps you decide on your career path and which skills to improve.

It is important to look at personal development approaches when planning a market-based career. It involves building a brand, showing off my unique qualifications, and learning from those who have more experience in my field. A powerful personal brand makes someone stand out in a crowded job market and draws the notice of possible employers.

To connect career goals with the market, you should take an active approach. It means regularly reflecting on and changing your work goals in response to changes in the market and yourself. If individuals keep up-to-date, respond to changes well, and map out their plans, they can expect both career stability and greater job satisfaction.

# Chapter 15: Harnessing Technology for Career Success

## Exploring Technological Tools

Technology has made a big difference in job searching, helping people find work in new ways. Using digital tools while searching for work is not only helpful but necessary for people hoping to keep a job during a recession. Because we live in a digital world, these resources keep getting better and more effective at joining job seekers with employers.

Most of these tools put job search platforms at the front, functioning as digital platforms for employers and job seekers to meet. Many people recognize sites like LinkedIn, Indeed, and Glassdoor, all of which offer features designed to make job searching easier. For example, LinkedIn is not only a platform for job searching; it also helps people network, speak with experts, and present their work experience with full profiles. LinkedIn gives people a great way to link up with recruiters and hiring managers in direct communication.

Since Indeed includes jobs from all kinds of industries and places, it has become the top choice for anyone in need of a job.

Job seekers can use the user-friendly site to filter by things like salary, where the job is, and how large the company is, making their search more personal. Meanwhile, Glassdoor lets job seekers learn about company cultures, what employees earn, and their experiences so they can decide which company to work for.

On top of these websites, new technologies have brought improvements and made searching for work easier and more productive. Using Trello or Asana makes it easier for people to track job applications, manage their search activities, and keep their schedules under control. They become more useful when a person is looking for work but needs to manage various tasks at the same time.

Slack and Microsoft Teams are now included in the list of useful tools for searching for a job. Thanks to these platforms, job seekers can easily connect with potential employers, have interviews, hold discussions, and make professional connections. Being able to speak with employers online overcomes the distance problem faced by job seekers.

In addition, the use of online learning sites has enabled people looking for jobs to develop new skills and keep up with changes in their jobs. Online learning websites such as Coursera and LinkedIn Learning give access to courses in many subjects, including technical ones and those focused on soft skills. Job seekers can show they are dedicated to learning new things by making use of these online assets.

Basically, using technology on the job means embracing the digital changes happening in the workforce. It includes realizing that learning digital skills supports making connections and gaining employment when the economy is tough. The advancements in technology mean job seekers need to use these tools in their job search to remain strong and successful in their careers. Effective technology use boosts your search for a job and also helps you get used to the digital requirements most employers now expect.

## Using Technology for Networking

With today's constant changes in our professional world, using technology is crucial to increasing and improving your professional network. Using the internet has led to different networking methods that allow connections across roles, locations, and professions. LinkedIn is at the heart of this upheaval, now linked to the idea of professional networking. It provides an interactive place to network with others, join different communities, and chat with people who might offer helpful new opportunities.

Virtual events offer another important way for professionals to connect. Hosting these events on Zoom or Microsoft Teams helps people all over the world take part without any distance issues. Using these meetings, professionals can talk about relevant topics, keep up with industry news, and form bonds that wouldn't have been possible without these events.

Twitter and Instagram help a great deal in making new industry connections. Twitter provides professionals with opportunities to interact, follow important people in their field, and join in on hashtag gatherings that might bring new connections and useful information. Instagram, mainly because of its visual appeal, gives creatives a place to display their work and find other people with similar interests. To get the most from these platforms, you should focus on building your brand in a way that reflects what you want from your career.

In addition, many tools, such as Slack and Discord, are now used to build online communities. In comparison to mainstream social media, these work best for target audiences by allowing them to repair and work together constantly. Getting involved on Slack channels or in Discord servers linked to what you do can give you useful help and form positive professional relationships.

To fully benefit from using these technologies, it helps to maintain an interactive presence on the internet. It includes taking part in conversations, posting useful information, and updating profiles whenever something new is added to your career. Also, using personal branding greatly improves your ability to use technology for network creation. Creating an online image that outlines someone's expertise and history of working can help draw the attention of potential collaborators and employers.

Moreover, knowing about the newest trends and technology is very important. Learning often by watching webinars, taking online classes, and listening to industry podcasts helps someone keep up with the latest tech trends. As a result, you grow your skills and have more possibilities to collaborate with others.

All in all, technology has made it much easier for people in the industry to reach out, acquire new knowledge, and improve themselves. Using various digital tools can help people grow professional networks that aid their career dreams and help them manage economic challenges. Adopting these technologies in forward-looking ways helps build a business network that makes a difference.

## Technology for Skill Enhancement

Because the job market is evolving so quickly, technology helps people improve their skills and remain valuable in their careers. Because industries keep changing, professionals need to use modern tools and platforms to keep up. Using technology for skill development opens up many learning opportunities that help individuals follow and even direct new industry trends.

Now, through online learning, we can learn new skills more flexibly than through classroom-based methods. Thanks to sites such as Coursera and LinkedIn Learning, people can get up-to-date training on topics like data analytics and creative writing when they have time outside work. Leading experts and universities from the industry are often involved in these platforms, so their content is always relevant and of top quality. When you can learn in your own time and go over difficult subjects, you grasp them better and become stronger in using new skills.

The use of virtual reality (VR) and augmented reality (AR) has become extremely important for developing skills. They allow students to practice and learn in a way that resembles what they will do in the real world, all without danger. VR is becoming popular in medicine and engineering because it helps improve precision and real-world experience. Through practice digitally, learners shape their abilities and feel sure that their skills are ready before working in real-world places.

Podcasts and webinars greatly help skill development. Professionals can use these formats to get the latest news and insights from experts all over the world. Following podcasts about your industry or tuning in to webinars can help you find creative answers to familiar challenges and encourage all to learn more every day.

It is extremely important to be aware of new technologies. As we improve our technology, we need to develop the skills we need to use it well. Professionals need to update their skills by reviewing tech news, going to education events, and engaging in workshops. Being informed about recent changes benefits individuals and also presents them as leaders and pioneers in their careers.

Networking and collaboration are important for building a career, and technology makes them much easier. Thanks to places like LinkedIn, you can link up with others and discuss ideas and helpful resources. Online meetings and forums allow experts to discuss important topics, swap insights, and miss out on partnering in the industry.

All in all, improving your skills with technology is important not just for adding skills but also for ensuring your career is durable and reliable in unpredictable work environments. Using modern technologies allows professionals to stay important and helpful in what they do. Skill enhancement takes time, as you need to stay committed to growing and adapting for your career to continue growing and bringing you joy.

## Staying Updated with Tech Trends

Being aware of technology is crucial nowadays to maintain a job that will not be affected by the next recession. As technology updates quickly, we need to be ready to learn and fit in with these changes. Since keeping up with new technologies is essential for the workforce, learning these trends can benefit anyone who wants a career that thrives.

You can stay current with technology by making deep use of the resources on the internet. By tuning into sector-related podcasts and webinars, you can easily learn about recent changes. These platforms typically include experts and leaders who provide insights into the uses of emerging technologies in several industries. Working through virtual reality training helps enhance understanding by allowing you to experience new and innovative tools and gadgets.

Staying informed is easy with help from technology news outlets and publications. Going through articles that come from respected sources on a regular basis will give you a clear understanding of the latest trends and innovations. Additionally, technology conferences and expos, either online or in person, give us a great chance to see and try out brand-new technologies. These happenings also offer great opportunities for professionals to meet each other, talk about their fields, and brainstorm about how technological progress will shape their profession.

It is very important to develop your skills always. When industries change, the abilities needed by their workers also change. Impartial evaluation of skills should be carried out routinely by professionals to find ways to grow. You can close the gap in your skills by registering for online courses or certifications that follow industry trends. With the help of LinkedIn Learning and Coursera, you have access to plenty of courses that help you develop the skills needed for the current job market.

Harvesting technology for instructional support will further increase learning and development. Tools and apps meant for project management, communication, and collaboration can drastically improve how quickly and well tasks are completed. In modern teams, being familiar with Trello, Asana, Slack, and Microsoft Teams makes working together and finishing tasks much more efficient.

The need to keep up with technology requires staying open to learning new things and being adaptable right through life. We must be ready for updates and be willing to use different approaches and tools. Adopting a view that supports perpetual learning and transformation can ensure your role security and also introduce you to new chances. Staying aware and adapting to new advancements can transform possible problems into important career steps, providing lasting success in the current economy.

## Examples of Tech-Driven Career Growth

Because technology is changing the workplace so quickly, multiple individuals have made their careers grow by using technology, and this demonstrates the broad influence of digital transformation everywhere. Based on these cases, it's obvious that technology use can greatly benefit a career by offering fresh, professional development paths.

Think about a marketer who moved into the world of data analytics. They realized that analytics was becoming critical for making strong marketing decisions. After signing up for online courses about data science and analytics, they learned how to interpret and represent data effectively. Using this new skill set, they played a big role in improving campaigns by using data about consumers and attaining increased promotions within their company.

Another good example is when a teacher took advantage of new digital tools to improve their teaching skills. Using interactive features and online courses, they boosted student engagement and made learning easier to reach. This strategy meant the educator's students did better, and the teacher became known as an influential person in educational technology, helping them lead digital curriculum activities.

The healthcare industry is home to many inspiring stories about using technology to move up in their jobs. First, the nurse worked in medical settings but then studied health informatics, which combines healthcare with information technology. Being able to use electronic health records opened the way for continuous improvements in how care was given using better medical data. Thanks to their knowledge of health informatics, their careers advanced, and healthcare became more smoothly delivered.

As a result of fintech growth, those willing to keep up with technology have new career opportunities in finance. For example, a financial advisor developed their skills by considering robo-advisors and blockchain in their field. By implementing these tools, they gave their clients top services, which helped increase both their clients and revenue in a constantly developing market.

With digital platforms making it possible, the gig economy has enabled plenty of people to try new directions in their careers. ICE professionals in different industries are using digital platforms to connect with clients around the world and improve their financial situation. Upwork and Fiverr allow graphic designers, writers, and developers in creative professions to find a larger audience and land projects that are important to them.

They reveal the major role technology can play in helping people advance in their careers. Informed about new technology and skillful, people can use the opportunities and careers they prefer in the digital era. Learning technology helps individuals and also encourages industry progress, which opens the door to additional growth and development.

# We'd Love Your Feedback!

**Title:**

**The Job Search Guide for Recession-Proof Careers**

**We'd Love Your Feedback!**

Thank you for reading **The Job Search Guide for Recession-Proof Careers.** I hope you found it insightful, practical, and inspiring.

If you enjoyed the book, we would be incredibly grateful if you could take a moment to leave a review on Amazon. Your feedback not only helps other readers discover the book, but it also supports our work and makes a big difference.

Scan the QR code below or visit the link to share your thoughts.

👉 Or visit: https://a.co/d/iCulJp5
👉 Or visit our website: https://synastbooks.com

With heartfelt thanks,
**JORDAN BLAKE**

www.ingramcontent.com/pod-product-compliance
Lightning Source LLC
Chambersburg PA
CBHW070550050426
42450CB00011B/2793